". . . a wonderful user-friendly book to help all of us realize our leadership potential, develop it, maintain our growth, and finish well."

JILL BRISCOE
Telling the Truth Ministries

"Leith Anderson is a passionate lover of the local church who has an enviable record of effective leadership in both the parish and among parachurch ministries. He knows sound leadership when he sees it and knows a great deal about the changing cultures which require revolutionary and transforming leadership. When Leith Anderson writes about leadership in the church, people listen!"

DR. GEORGE K. BRUSHABER
President, Bethel College & Seminary

". . . should be required reading for anyone planning to enter the ministry. Way beyond platitudes—this is the real thing."

BOB BUFORD
Founder and Chairman of Leadership Network

"Regardless of your church's geographical location, size, maturity, or culture, *Leadership That Works* will add tremendous value to your professional and personal ministry."

KIRBYJON H. CALDWELL
Senior Pastor, Windsor Village United Methodist Church

"Too often leadership does not work, for leadership must work in practice. Leith introduces his reader to the real world—confronting failure, disillusionment, and difficulties—but winning through. Here is a practical guide from one who has been there and by God's grace has proved it can work!"

DR. CLIVE CALVER
President, World Relief

"This is one of those rare books that should be read by every Christian who wants to lead effectively, not merely for personal fulfillment, but for the advancement of God's kingdom!"

DR. PAUL A. CEDAR
Chairman, Mission America

". . . an amazingly practical yet biblical guide for all Christian leaders. Leith exposes now-obsolete concepts, reinforces still viable ones, and inspires awesome hope by showing how God seems to be doing His greatest thing ever around the world right now."

EVELYN CHRISTENSON
Founder and President, United Prayer Ministry

"Leith Anderson is one of the most important voices for church leadership that is both splendidly spiritual and profoundly practical. He has applied the totality of his giftedness as a pastor, thinker, writer, and culture-watching futurist to church leadership."

JOHN R. CORTS
President, Billy Graham Evangelistic Association

"The only leadership that matters is leadership that works; everything else is pure theory. Leith Anderson has again given us an extremely practical look into the issue of leadership by drawing upon his rich background, his inquiring mind, and his down-to-earth application of the obvious implications of effective leadership in the 21st century."

BILL CREWS
President, Golden Gate Baptist Theological Seminary

"In a world of changing rules, Anderson shares an intensively practical book that addresses much more than just leadership."

WILLIAM M. EASUM
President, Easum, Bandy & Associates

"This book provides the leader with a path through the complexity of contemporary culture. It gives the reader both practical tools and hope for relevant ministry now."

DALE E. GALLOWAY
Dean, Beeson Leadership Center

"Leith Anderson offers a unique blend of common sense, practical wisdom, personal experience, statistical insights, and prophetic foresight for Christian leaders. He doesn't just talk about his successes, which are apparent, but also his failures, which are not so apparent. This allows perceptive leaders to learn what should not be done, as well as what should be done."

PASTOR JOEY JOHNSON
Senior Pastor, The House of the Lord

". . . invigoratingly insightful and helpful. It's a must read for every Christian who takes leadership seriously."

WALT KALLESTAD
Community of Joy

"Too often we pastors are caught up in what we think we should be doing, and we miss the big picture. Leith Anderson teaches us to stop and understand where we need to be moving toward and why."

DR. CHARLES LOWERY
Senior Pastor, Hoffmantown Church

"When I think of Leith Anderson I think of leadership. He is a pastor who 'understands our times and knows what to do' (1 Chron. 12:32). His own trusted leadership works, and his hope-filled counsel for leaders everywhere deserves our fullest attention."

STEPHEN A. MACCHIA
President, Vision New England

"Today's fast and furious world has raised numerous obstacles for leaders who desire to finish well: mind-boggling complexity, barren busyness, multiple options, overwhelming competition, relentless stress, and impossible expectations. However, Leith Anderson comes alongside leaders to boldly give hope and direction for significant ministry in the 21st century."

AUBREY MALPHURS
Professor & Department Chairman of Field Education, Dallas Theological Seminary

"As any leader soon learns, leading is hard! Anderson acknowledges this fact and helps us realize why leading the church is actually getting harder. Using practical, relevant anecdotes, Anderson shows how the escalating rate of change in the culture and the development of more options challenge ministry leaders in unexpected ways. For the seasoned leader and for the student in ministry training, this book will be an encouraging resource."

SCOTTIE MAY
Assistant Professor, Department of Christian Formation and Ministry, Wheaton College

"There is no one better positioned to show us how to lead in the 21st century than Leith Anderson. I suggest you read *Leadership That Works* as soon as possible and begin putting its insights into practice immediately. You'll be glad you did!"

DR. GARY L. MCINTOSH
Professor of Christian Ministry and Leadership, Talbot School of Theology, Biola University

". . . both a manual and a diary. Leith Anderson gives us access to both his heart and his mind. Through his writing we can all be mentored by one of America's most insightful and effective leaders."

ERWIN R. MCMANUS
Lead Pastor, MOSAIC

"Leith Anderson invites us to shape our leadership to fit our particular gifts in our unique context. For Leith, leadership is not one's personal skill or gift—it is composed of hard work, sensitivity, and a willingness to respond when God calls."

LOREN B. MEAD
Founding President of Alban Institute

"Incredibly valuable, this is vintage Leith Anderson doing what he does best: building lighthouses of insight along the shifting shoreline of rapid change in culture and congregations."

HERB MILLER
Editor, The Parish Paper

"If you're feeling stressed by the pressure of Christian leadership, you may not feel you have time to read this book. But do yourself a big favor—buy it and read it. Leith brilliantly tells us what's happening today and how to respond."

KEVIN A. MILLER
Editor-at-Large, LEADERSHIP

"It makes sense that if our world is changing, then those who lead it and their style should change as well. Boiled down. Bottom line. That's the style of advice Leith Anderson offers. No more

excuses—just help and direction for leading . . . now."

ELISA MORGAN
President and CEO, MOPS International

"More than a handbook of established leadership principles, this book provides astute analysis of our present culture, a vibrant hope in the possibilities and opportunities ahead, and creative answers to the hard questions facing those called to leadership in the new millennium. Get this book!"

THE REV. CHARLES H. MURPHY III
Rector, All Saints Episcopal Church

"This visionary pastor and speaker makes you feel as if you can be an effective leader and make a difference in God's kingdom."

BOBBIE PATTERSON
Associate Executive Director, Women's Missionary Union

"With his fascinating facility for connecting us with the increasingly complex realities of our changing present and the daunting challenges of the future, Leith Anderson proposes fresh paradigms for Christian leadership—sound, stretching, sometimes troubling, but always alight with honest insight, bright hope, and promise. The last two pages are worth the price of the book."

GENERAL PAUL A. RADER (RETIRED)
Former International Leader of the Salvation Army

"Leith Anderson is a leader. In this extremely valuable book he passes on insights that can help others lead as well. If you're only going to read ten books this year, by all means, make this one of them."

HADDON ROBINSON
Harold John Ockenga Professor of Preaching, Gordon-Conwell Theological Seminary

"A must read! Anderson writes about the leadership matrix in a post-modern world where change is the only constant and the leadership directive is 'fix it before it breaks.' This is Leith's best work yet!"

MICHAEL SLAUGHTER
Pastor, Ginghamsburg Church

"Whereas some writers glorify pastoral leadership without discussing its pressures and pitfalls, Leith Anderson realistically describes hard steps to pastoral success. Some write

about visionary leadership as though all the pastor has to do is to create a wonderful vision and an operative mission statement; but Leith Anderson takes the leader into the trenches to describe what must be done to win the battle."

ELMER L. TOWNS
Dean, School of Religion, Liberty University

"Pastors and parachurch leaders should read this book to explode the myths about church leadership and chart some of their course for future ministry."

DAVE TRAVIS
Director of Interventionist Networks, Leadership Network

"Pastoring a dynamic, cutting-edge church is an incredible challenge today. Leith Anderson not only does it, but he explains it so clearly that others can do it too."

C. PETER WAGNER
Chancellor, Wagner Leadership Institute

Leadership
THAT WORKS

*Hope and Direction for Church and
Parachurch Leaders in Today's Complex World*

Leith
Anderson

 BETHANY HOUSE PUBLISHERS
Minneapolis, Minnesota 55438
www.bethanyhouse.com

Published by Bethany House Publishers
A Ministry of Bethany Fellowship International
11400 Hampshire Avenue South
Minneapolis, Minnesota 55438
www.bethanyhouse.com

Printed in the United States of America by
Bethany Press International, Minneapolis, Minnesota 55438

Library of Congress Cataloging-in-Publication Data

Anderson, Leith, 1944–
    Leadership that works / by Leith Anderson.
       p.   cm.
    Includes bibliographical references.
    ISBN 1–55661–994–4
    1. Christian leadership. I. Title.
BV652.1.A525   1999
253—dc21

99–6592
CIP

To my seven mentors

Charles W. Anderson . . . father
Austin Chapman . . . layleader
Robert P. Dugan Jr. . . . junior high youth pastor
Jack Estep . . . senior pastor
Vernon Grounds . . . seminary president
Charles Horne . . . theology professor
Lyle Schaller . . . consultant

LEITH ANDERSON is senior pastor of Wooddale Church in the Minneapolis suburb of Eden Prairie, Minnesota, and has also been serving as interim president of Denver Seminary. He is a graduate of Bradley University (B.A.), Denver Seminary (M.Div.), and Fuller Theological Seminary (D.Min.).

Although he is known nationally as an author, speaker, and educator, his first love is the local church and its people. For over twenty years his preaching, vision, and leadership have helped guide Wooddale Church through a process of change and growth, putting it on the cutting edge to meet the spiritual needs of its people and to reach out to the surrounding community.

Anderson has written five books with Bethany House Publishers:

A Church for the 21st Century
Dying for Change
Leadership That Works
Praying to the God You Can Trust
Winning the Values War in a Changing Culture

Contents

Chapter 1

What's Happening That's So Different?

Too-Old Tom

Tom is a third-generation parish minister who has served five congregations in four states over thirty-five years. When he graduated from seminary at age twenty-five he was called "cutting edge," "maverick," and "brave young pastor." He won the seminary's preaching award because of his classical oratorical skills, and he built his ministry by perfecting those skills in fifty Sunday morning sermons every year and by making more than one thousand pastoral calls and appointments yearly.

But then the unimaginable happened. Three members of his church board took Tom out for lunch and asked for his resignation. Tom listened in shock as they laid out the details. He would have six months to seek a call from another church. During that time no one else from the church would know that he had been asked to leave. If after that period of time he hadn't been called to another church, he would be given six months' severance salary plus coverage of his family's health insurance for up to eighteen additional months or until he started another job with benefits.

Not until after lunch did Tom realize that the whole conversation centered on the "how" of his leaving rather than the "why." The men never clearly told him why they wanted his resignation.

At the regular monthly meeting of the entire board a week later, Tom asked why he was being asked to leave. In a tense and uncomfortable exchange, the board gave several vague answers: "This is a new day in church life and we need new leadership," the chairman said. "Younger adults prefer a more conversational style of preaching," another man added. "We want a pastor who focuses more on vision than visitation," someone else said. "We're losing our young people to other churches." "The new independent church down the road is attracting our members." "Many people in the church would prefer more informal but more intense worship."

Tom didn't fully understand some of the comments, especially the one about informal but intense worship, so he drew his own conclusion. Even though no one said, "You're too old and we want a younger pastor," that was Tom's interpretation.

During the next three weeks Tom preached his best. He also increased his number of home and hospital calls by 20 percent, in the hope that he might hear something from other church members that would help him understand what was happening and maybe even build up loyalty in the case of a church-wide showdown.

He also called his new district superintendent. The superintendent agreed to intervene and invoke denominational policy if Tom insisted, but he thought it would be better for Tom to leave quietly and gracefully. "After all," he said, "if you win you lose. What are your chances of effectively ministering in a church where the entire board wants you out? Why don't you let me recommend you to some other churches?"

So Tom agreed to begin the interview process.

In the past, search committees had always been delighted to have Tom as a candidate. He'd had his pick of the best churches. But this time was different. Now he was being recommended to churches no one else wanted and ones that didn't really want him. Again, no one said, "You're too old," but several came close when they said they were looking for a pastor "who will celebrate a twenty-fifth anniversary here." Tom found such comments interesting since none of those churches had kept a pastor more than seven years in the past century.

Tom had not expected to conclude his ministerial career in this way. He assumed that the combination of his preaching skills and faithful leadership would only lead to better and better churches. He'd been sure that one day he would have to choose between a denominational leadership role, teaching at the denominational seminary, or preaching until he died. Instead it was beginning to look as if he would have to seek secular employment until his denomination's pension kicked in. How could someone considered to be on the "cutting edge" such a short time ago all of a sudden be too dull to "cut it" in the ministry? Tom wondered.

Mainline Mary

As a child Mary not only dreamed of being a preacher someday but she practiced it. At age six she began gathering together the neighborhood children for pretend church services. She would set up the chairs in rows, play religious songs on her mom's tape player, read from the Bible, preach about Noah and the Ark, and serve Communion with Kool-Aid and animal crackers.

Even though Mary had never met a woman minister, her dream did not flicker or fade. And even though college friends convinced her she would be better off in social work or teaching, her desire didn't change.

She majored in elementary education at one of her denomination's liberal arts colleges, participated actively in student ministries and the life of the campus church, met and married Charles, and taught third grade for two years before becoming a stay-at-home mom for the next eleven years. By then her husband's career was well established and the children were in school all day, so Mary decided to go to seminary.

Three years later Mary completed a master of divinity degree with a 4.0 grade point average. She won the "Golden

Pulpit" award as the best preacher in her graduating class. At last her dreams were coming true. Or so she thought. Her denomination requires every pastoral search committee to be made up of equal numbers of men and women and to consider fully and fairly female candidates. Mary had four interviews, but each church chose a man. Gender was never an issue, they said. The men were more qualified. Had more experience. Were better suited to the pastoral profile. Mary received several job offers, but they were from large affluent churches seeking children's pastors, not from churches wanting to hire a preaching pastor.

Mary didn't give up, but she knew she had to face a troubling reality: the churches willing to consider her were the ones others didn't want. They were two-point country charges (where the pastor is responsible for two churches), inner city mini-cathedrals with few people and deteriorating buildings, or churches seeking to fulfill political and theological agendas that Mary didn't espouse. Mary just wanted to preach and be a pastor, as she had been called and trained to do. Instead she discovered that there was a large gap between the official rules of the denomination and the actual practices of the churches.

Rural Ralph

Ralph has attended First Church his entire life. He is a pillar of the community and a pillar of the church. His parents are buried in the church cemetery. His wife has been the church organist for thirty-eight years. His son and daughter-in-law lead the youth group of four teenagers. Although church rules require deacons to rotate off the governing board after three years, Ralph attends all the meetings during his sabbatical year and then is reelected to another three-year term. Except for his driving trip to Alaska and his hospitalization after a tractor accident, Ralph has never missed a board meeting. People at church say, "Pastors come and pastors go, but Ralph is at church forever." That is an especially interesting statement since the current pastor has been at the church for fifteen years and the predecessor pastored there for twelve years. The Reverend Theodore MacDonald, who died when Ralph was seven years old, served First Church for forty-three years.

Not much has changed since Ralph was a boy. Same building. Same parsonage. Same rotary telephone in the pastor's study. Same basic order of service.

But the people are changing. Almost every young person leaves town after high school graduation and never returns. Some go to college, some join the military, and some find jobs in the city. The few who do return to town don't return to First Church; they attend more contemporary churches in the county seat, a town with a population of thirty thousand about sixteen miles down the interstate.

Newcomers at First Church are few, and none come from the longtime families of the area. They are city people who fall into one of three categories: those who have jobs that allow them to work from home; those who are willing to put up with an hour-and-a-half commute twice a day so their children can grow up in the country; or retirees. All three groups have different expectations, and to Ralph their ideas for change seem endless.

Ralph is a nice guy who likes people, especially those who love to stand around and talk about the weather, fishing, hunting, and politics. But he doesn't like newcomers who want to change his church. Three recent issues have been especially troubling to him:

- Newcomers want representation on the church board, but none of them attend Sunday evening services. They say they are too busy, but Ralph thinks they are uncommitted. "It's bad enough that they don't get home from work in time to come to Wednesday evening prayer meeting," moans Ralph, "but they have no excuse for missing Sunday evenings."

- Newcomers insist on higher quality music. One even suggested hiring a part-time organist to replace Ralph's wife. Ralph cleared this up in a hurry, explaining that "our present organist is a fine person who has faithfully played for thirty-eight years, and we don't pay anybody to do anything around here except the pastor. This is a volunteer organization where people give their time, talents, and treasures."

- Newcomers keep trying to change the service times. They want the Sunday morning service to start at ten or ten-thirty instead of eleven. Ralph is against it. He explains that the services have begun at eleven o'clock for the past hundred years, and they will begin at eleven o'clock for the next hundred years. He even quoted the Bible to make his point, saying, "Jesus is the same yesterday, today, and forever, so there's no good reason to worship him an hour earlier." What he doesn't admit is that he once told his brother that he wished NFL games would start later or that church services would end before the kickoff. If he ever let it be known that he wanted an earlier service, there would be no stopping all the changes the city people would introduce. As Ralph says, "Let the camel's nose in the tent and before long you'll have the whole stinkin' animal in your house."

While Ralph is struggling with people who want his rural church to function like a city church, his cousin is the newcomer at a city church that functions like a rural church. The difference isn't as much ZIP code and geography as it is approach to church and community life.

Bishop Bob

Bob was chosen as bishop because of his skills and experience. He holds a Ph.D. in classics from the University of Edinburgh, and he is an exceptional leader. He was a navy chaplain during the Vietnam War, a parish rector in Virginia for nearly twenty years, dean of All Saints Seminary, and is well known for his wonderful combination of communication skills, godliness, and humility. He is everything anyone would want a bishop to be. It's a good thing, because many people think he has an impossible job.

Within his diocese, there is a deep schism over the ordination of women, the place of homosexuals in the church, and the expenditure of denominational funds for social and political causes. The conservatives (who prefer to be called "orthodox") are very conservative. The liberals (who prefer to be called "progressive") are very liberal.

The average age of the parishioners in his denomination is

sixty-four years and climbing. The average church has 178 members, but only about 70 attend worship on Sunday mornings, and even that number is declining. Forty percent of denominational employees have been laid off due to budget cuts during the past triennium. These and other statistics point to a pattern of precipitous decline. Thirty years ago the churches failed to reach or retain the younger generation. Now these churches are dying of old age. If the trend continues, over half of the existing churches will die in the next twenty-five years.

At the same time there is a cadre of churches that are growing rapidly and attracting large numbers of young adults and young families. These churches are theologically conservative and methodologically maverick. They don't use the denominational name on their signs, in their advertising, or on church literature. In fact, if no one asks, they don't tell. The services have a definite interdenominational but nonecumenical flavor. For example, they allow anyone to receive Communion, but they won't allow clergy from fraternal denominations to serve Communion. Both practices are in direct defiance of church law. They allow speaking in tongues, but they don't allow practicing homosexuals into leadership positions.

The new bishop is under heavy pressure to intervene and stop the "heretical" practices of the maverick churches. Meanwhile, the maverick churches are withholding denominational contributions because the bishop won't crack down on the "heresies" of the liberals.

Some say it's all a matter of law. Just read the law and apply it. But the bishop knows it's not that simple. For one thing, laws are more about church politics and who shows up for meetings than about tradition, the Bible, or what is right. As a result, many of the laws have been changed over recent years.

The bishop realizes that if he supports the liberals he is backing a dying breed, which may mean the end of his church. On the other hand, if he backs the conservatives they may take over and split the denomination. Besides, he wonders, do the people attracted to the new churches know or care enough about the denomination to look for a church of the same denomination if they ever move? And what chance is there that they will give substantial amounts of money or name the

denomination in their wills when they aren't even sure to what
denomination they belong?

What's a bishop to do?

Faithful Fred

Fred worked his way up from the bottom. First he was a
pastor in a member denomination of the National Association
of Churches. He started attending the annual conventions and
was eventually rewarded with a committee assignment. He
worked so hard on the by-laws committee that they elected him
chairman and later promoted him to the resolutions committee.
From the resolutions committee, he was given a post on the
prestigious program committee and eventually on the executive
committee. He never missed a meeting. He never arrived late.
He fulfilled every assignment given to him. Fred even gave to
the association and prayed regularly for its pastors and
churches, all while serving full-time as a local church pastor in
West Virginia.

When the president of the association approached him with
a job offer, Fred was truly surprised. For the same salary he was
receiving, he could move to the association headquarters in
Washington, D.C., and assume the post of church relations director. He gladly accepted the offer and worked very hard at his
new assignment. Although not especially creative, he was always dependable. Fred wrote reports, called churches, answered questions, and represented the association as a true loy-
alist.

Seven years later the president of the association suffered a
debilitating stroke. He retained the presidency with full salary
for three years, but never came to the office because he was unable to speak or write. Fred functioned as acting interim president during those difficult thirty-six months, and the association ran smoothly under his leadership. Although there was an
operations deficit each of those years, Fred chose not to lay off
any employees because they had sacrificially served for many
years and the right thing to do was to keep them on at any price.

At the annual convention Fred gave one of the best speeches
of his career in honor of his outgoing and disabled boss. Inter-

estingly, he never mentioned any accomplishments of the president, but he used the word "faithful" eighty-seven times in twenty-three minutes. He concluded with a quote from Jesus: "Well done, good and faithful servant." His display of love and loyalty greatly impressed the presidential search committee, and at their meeting the next morning Fred was added to the short list of presidential candidates.

After another six months of résumés, references, and interviews, Fred was recommended to the board of directors as the next association president. The vote was six "yea" and three "nay." Robertson Sinclair, a young lawyer and layman on the search committee, explained his "nay" vote: "Fred is a good man. I would hire him to work in my law firm. He is loyal. He does what he is asked to do. He is faithful. But he's not the kind of leader this association needs in the twenty-first century. Faithfulness is simply not enough. We need effectiveness."

Associate Alice

Alice never wanted a church job. Her goals in life were simple and clear: First, complete a degree in elementary music education; second, get a good job teaching grade school music; third, get married; fourth, quit her job; fifth, have children.

Like many people's life goals, Alice's didn't go the way she expected. The year she graduated from college there weren't many teaching jobs available in Colorado. She loved the Rocky Mountain West and didn't want to move to rural North Dakota where a contract was available for a combined class of first and second graders and no music component. Besides, she figured her chances of meeting "Mr. Right" were greater in Denver than in a small town. So she kept her college job waiting on tables at the Brown Palace Hotel, moving from part time to full time. With tips, she actually made more money as a server than she would have made as a teacher. The difference was that she had to work summers.

Alice became involved in a Baptist church with an average attendance of 650 in the worship service. She liked the pastor, the music, and the singles group, which was surprisingly large and active for the size of the congregation. When the chairman of the Christian education committee met Alice and learned about her background, he asked if she would be interested in starting a children's choir the following September. She accepted the offer and was a great success. The children loved Alice; the parents loved Alice; the whole church loved Alice. She was so popular that when the part-time children's pastor resigned, the search committee decided during the first hour of the first meeting that Alice should be offered the job. Although flattered, she said no. She explained that there just weren't enough hours in the week to keep her full-time job and work part-time at the church. Besides, she wanted to remain available for an elementary teaching job.

The search committee wouldn't take no for an answer. They talked to the senior pastor and called a special meeting of the church board. Within a week they were back offering Alice full-time employment as director of children's ministry and music. The chairman of the search committee researched starting teachers' salaries in the nearby school district and arrived at a salary package that would pay Alice what she would receive as a teacher plus another third (as compensation for the summer months she would have had off as a teacher). Alice accepted.

During the next two years Alice could do no wrong. The church licensed her as a minister, offered to pay her way through seminary as a part-time student, and gave her the new title of Associate Pastor for Children. The Sunday school grew, the number of adult volunteers doubled, and the church began to build a reputation for having the best children's program around. During those two years the whole church grew more than 20 percent, and Alice received 100 percent of the credit.

Then the offers started to come. A Presbyterian church in California offered double her salary and two full-time assistants. An Assemblies of God church in Missouri offered her a first-class airline ticket to fly out and take a look—no obligation, of course. A seminary in Texas offered her a full-time teaching position as part of their new master of arts in children's ministry degree, plus a commitment to pay for her education to earn a doctorate.

Alice had never even wanted to be a church leader, but for

some reason the whole church world seemed to be beating a path to her door.

What's Happening?

Twenty-first century leadership in the church and other religious organizations isn't what it used to be. It's as if all the rules have changed. How can someone like Tom go from cutting edge to out-of-date in so few years? What should Mary do when the official rules of her denomination vary so greatly from the actual practice of its churches? Is Ralph supposed to change his leadership style and his church just because the community is switching from rural to exurban? Is schism the only "solution" for the church that Bob so dearly loves but is struggling to lead through a minefield of dangers, many of which are the consequence of bad or delayed decisions by former leaders? Isn't faithfulness enough for Fred? Does he have to buy into modern business definitions of success, or can he measure his life by his unwavering allegiance to God? And then there's Alice. Because she is good with children, and children's ministry is hot, she is considered the paramount example of Christian leadership success even though she's doing something she never planned to do. What is happening anyway?

On the sad side are the good people who haven't heard what is happening and so they just keep trying harder and harder in the old ways.

On the bright side are those leaders—both young and old—who understand how the changes in society affect Christian leadership. Not all things need to change, but they know how to live out changeless Christian truths and values in a changing culture.

Cultural changes are not new in our era. During the transition between the reigns of King Saul and King David, at about the turn of the first millennium B.C., civil war ripped apart the nation of Israel. Tribes, clans, families, and individuals had to decide which leader to follow, and it was not an easy decision. After all, Saul had been chosen for the throne by God himself and anointed by God's prophet Samuel. Who would dare turn against God's anointed? Not even David was willing to attack

Saul personally. "The Lord forbid that I should lay a hand on the Lord's anointed" (1 Samuel 26:11), he stated.

To turn against Saul was more than an act of treason against the king; it was an act of rebellion against God. But David also had been chosen by God to be king of Israel and was anointed by God's prophet Samuel. How could any committed Hebrew not recognize David as the Lord's choice?

It came down to a seemingly impossible decision between God's leadership choice for yesterday and God's leadership choice for tomorrow. Most people didn't get it. Most didn't know how to choose properly. But buried in a list of less-than-interesting names and numbers is an obscure statement about an ancient group of people, the men of Issachar, who "understood the times and knew what Israel should do—200 chiefs, with all their relatives under their command." There weren't many of them, only 200 in a nation of more than one million citizens, but they had followers, and they made a difference because they knew what to do.

Although today's names and places are different, something similar is happening. As we leave behind the twentieth century and launch into the twenty-first, we too must decide between old ways and new ways. It is not that the old ways were bad; they weren't. In fact, many were anointed by God. Nor are the new ways bad; they may be anointed by God. The difficulty comes in discerning between what God blessed yesterday and what God will bless tomorrow. Many will not understand, but some modern men and women, like those leaders of the tribe of Issachar, already know what the church of Jesus Christ should do in the new millennium.

Chapter 2

Why Is Leadership So Hard?

PETER DRUCKER was speaking to a group of senior ministers from large churches when he said, "Other than president of the United States, the three most difficult jobs in America today are president of a large university, administrator of a large general hospital, and pastor of a large church."[1]

These jobs are difficult in organizations of any size because they deal with diverse groups of people and require an unusual mix of skills. University presidents usually come from the academic world and have earned doctorates in specific disciplines. They are scholars in their own right. In addition, they are fundraisers with donors, managers with faculty (which may be unionized or at least operate with union-like rules), employers to staff, administrators with students, advocates with accrediting and government agencies, customer relations experts with parents, and a strange combination of employees and visionaries with their boards of trustees. Hospital administrators deal with medical professionals, nonmedical employees, patients and their families, accrediting and government regulatory agencies, insurance companies and health maintenance organizations, donors, and trustees. Pastors are expected to be biblical and theological scholars, business administrators, counselors, public speakers, fund-raisers, and visionaries, plus lead a personal life that is consistent with the values of the church. All of these positions have a high risk of lawsuits, public scrutiny, and involuntary termination due to alleged inability to provide the expected leadership in rapidly changing institutions.

What makes these roles so difficult is the wide range of skills needed to relate well to the variety of people who are part of the organization. The hospital administrator who is brilliant with finances but has terrible people skills probably isn't good enough. The college president who is loved by parents and hated by faculty won't last long. The pastor who is a captivating public speaker but can't get along with the church board will soon run into disaster.

Leadership has always been difficult. It was hard for Moses, David, Paul, Martin Luther, and Abraham Lincoln. Are some leadership positions more difficult than others? Of course. Is leadership more difficult now than it used to be? In many ways, yes. In fact, that may be part of the reason so many potential leaders are reluctant to accept leadership responsibilities. The job just isn't worth all the work.

Understanding the challenges of leadership will not make it easy, but it will go a long way toward putting the difficulties into proper perspective. The following descriptions do not apply to every situation, but they illustrate why leadership of Christian organizations is so difficult.

Churches Are Aging

The average life cycle of a church is a top-flattened bell curve:

Birth Stage (growing)	1–12 years
Plateau Stage (stable)	12–50 years
Decline Stage (dying)	51–70+ years

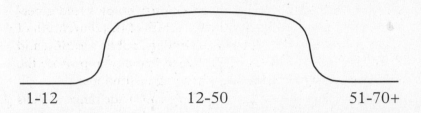

1-12   12-50   51-70+

Not all churches fit this description. All Saints Episcopal Church in Pawley's Island, South Carolina, for example, is older than the United States of America and by far the largest and healthiest it has ever been. This dynamic congregation mentors other Episcopal churches, trains clergy, and continues reaching people. When the Lake Avenue Congregational Church in Pasadena, California, celebrated its one hundredth anniversary, it had been growing for a century. Not every year ended with more people than the previous year, but every decade did. All ten of them. All Saints and Lake Avenue are wonderful exceptions, but they *are* exceptions. Most century-old congregations are not growing. In fact, a significant number of churches close before they celebrate their centennial.

In 1998 the metropolitan area of Minneapolis and St. Paul had 2,190 churches for approximately 2.5 million people. Eighteen and a half percent of these churches were founded in the nineteenth century and are over one hundred years old. Eighty-seven and a half percent were started before 1990. The average age of Twin Cities churches is fifty-six years. Comparing the life cycle concept to the ages of these churches reveals statistics that are not surprising—in 1997, 68 percent of the area churches had reached a plateau, 24 percent were declining, and 8 percent were growing.[2]

The age of a church may be measured not only by the founding date of the congregation but also by the average age of its members. Often the two go together. The Presbyterian Church U.S.A. has many older congregations and the average age of its members is sixty-four.[3]

Churches don't live indefinitely, any more than church

members do. The New Testament churches of Antioch, Philippi, Galatia, Corinth, and Jerusalem don't exist today in direct succession of the New Testament congregations of two thousand years ago. Like people, churches age, get sick, and die.

As we end the twentieth century and begin the twenty-first, North America is experiencing a resurgence of church planting, especially among independent churches and evangelical denominations. These new churches will have a powerful influence on religious life for the next generation. In fact, denominations that fail to start new churches will risk the loss of vitality, significant downsizing, and possible death.

Most churches in existence today are older than twelve years and have already reached the plateau stage or have started to decline. Leadership of these churches is even more difficult. They tend to suffer from one or more common maladies:

1. *Longing.* People want to go back to the "good old days" without having to adapt to new realities.

2. *Fear.* People want to guard against outside corrupting influences so they create a fortress mentality to keep newcomers out.

3. *Unfriendly.* Aging members don't welcome newcomers unless they are born or married into member families.

4. *Misplaced priorities.* People are more committed to the church building than to the church mission.

5. *Dysfunction.* Church leaders do not behave in a healthy manner.

6. *Inadequate finances.* People are unwilling or unable to sacrifice to provide necessary funds.

7. *Complacency.* People are satisfied with the status quo.

8. *Desperation.* Leaders don't know what to do.

9. *Aging.* Members are dying and not being replaced with new members or new babies.

10. *Sociological shift.* Members have moved from the neighborhood and the church is unable or unwilling to reach out to those who live nearby.

11. *Conflict.* The people within the church fight with each other.

12. *Lack of vision.* Leaders don't know what they want or can't agree on it.

13. *Incompetence.* The church lacks leaders who know what to do and know how to do it.

14. *Spiritual collapse.* The church has lost its biblical and spiritual foundation and really is no longer a church.

15. *Sin.* The congregation has been overcome with spiritual cancer that has disabled it and is killing it.

Leading an older church can be like being the personal trainer for a man who is old, out of shape, and has bad dietary habits. It's a difficult job, but that's no reason not to do it. Even though he will never win an Olympic medal, it's still possible to help the man become all he can and should be. The same is true of aging churches. They have special challenges that require special skills and efforts, but they can be led to renewal and renaissance. When it happens, they are delighted by the changes. Since most churches are aging, we need leaders who understand the challenges, will develop the skills, and are willing to put in the effort.

What applies to churches also applies to many parachurch organizations, though often for different reasons. As they age, they require new leadership skills. The life cycle is probably shorter for most noneducational parachurch organizations.

The aging issue for parachurch organizations focuses on a few key areas: (1) aging donor base that might disapprove of new methods and ministries; (2) bequests that financially underwrite current operations and thereby render the organization unaccountable to current and future constituencies; (3) board of directors more focused on guaranteeing the organization remains intact than on making sure it fulfills its mission.

Organizations Reward Dysfunction

The senior pastor of a mainline church in the Rocky Mountain West announced his resignation. The associate pastor decided to apply for the senior position but was unanimously turned down by the search committee elected by the congregation. The associate pastor and some of his friends mounted

a campaign to unseat the search committee and force the congregation to vote him into the office of senior pastor. Petitions
were circulated. Phone calls were made. Personal criticisms of
search committee members were circulated. Supporters wore
red clothes to church events along with campaign buttons that
said, "WEAR RED IF YOU WANT FRED." Fred even wore
red vestments at the altar each Sunday, even though the color
did not fit the season or liturgy. The results were impressive.
The search committee was forced out, the senior pastor left,
former members of the search committee and a significant
number of other church members drifted away to other
churches in the community, and Fred became the new senior
minister.

Whether Fred stays six months or sixty years, he's in for a
difficult ride because he landed himself a church that rewards
dysfunction. Inappropriate behavior is not only tolerated, it is
the most effective way to get something done. Sooner or later,
these methods will be used against Fred and every other leader
of a dysfunctional church.

Perhaps the most commonly rewarded dysfunction is the
empowerment of the wrong people. Individuals who would be
fired from their jobs or thrown in jail if they exhibited such
behavior in the larger community are allowed to threaten,
intimidate, control, and manipulate in the church. Their tactics
include claims that "I know a number of people in the church
who feel exactly the way I do about this situation." Seldom are
they willing to say who the other persons are. This is almost
always a sign of lying or manipulation. Healthy people speak for
themselves and don't need to enlist an invisible army to back
them up. While some are outwardly aggressive and attacking,
more are passively aggressive, undermining the church and its
leadership more by what they are against than by what they are
for.

I'm not saying we shouldn't allow disturbed people into the
church, but we shouldn't allow disturbed people to disrupt the
church. The difficulty comes when churches reward dysfunction rather than help people overcome it. Churches with unhealthy reward systems escalate problems by engaging the
entire congregation in the conflict, allowing minorities to rule

under the pretext of Christian compassion and rewarding dysfunctional members by appointing them to committees or electing them to governing boards. Where there should be confrontation and loving discipline, there is often accommodation and reinforcement. The problem is compounded when the reward system is perpetuated over many years and multiple generations. The result is that the church keeps the dissenters and loses the happy, healthy people to other churches. Most healthy Christians have a time limit and a tolerance level for unchristian and unhealthy attitudes and behavior. They prefer to go elsewhere rather than to stretch these limits. Newcomers may visit, but they seldom stay under stressful circumstances. They've seen enough dysfunction in their families and at work; they certainly aren't looking to become part of a sick church.

Churches don't have to be old to have an unhealthy reward system. And the reward structure isn't always built by the people; it may be built by the leader. When I was a young, new senior pastor in a Colorado church of two hundred, the board proposed selling the parsonage and allowing me to buy a house. Due to escalating real estate values, many churches were abandoning ownership of parsonages, and many pastors were buying houses to build equity toward home ownership in retirement. It was a win-win situation. Unfortunately a few dissenters turned a routine decision into an opportunity for criticism and conflict. They accused me of wanting to get rich at church expense. They wondered what they would do when the next pastor needed a place to live and the parsonage had been sold. Eventually there was a church vote that overwhelmingly approved the sale. However, I had spiritual concern for my critics and declined the offer. My family set aside our house plans and stayed in the church parsonage. In some ways it was a good decision, because it communicated to the congregation that I really wasn't greedy. On the other hand, it enabled a small minority to prevail over the large majority of the congregation and established (or reinforced) an unhealthy precedent of rewarding negative criticism and dissent.[4]

Leadership is more difficult in churches and organizations that reward dysfunctional behavior. The behavior may include gossip, failure to follow godly leaders, immorality, mismanagement or misappropriation of funds, nepotism, heresy, or pervasive incompetence.

Effective leadership may require a whole new value system that includes retraining the way people think and establishing a healthy reward system. In extreme cases, the leader may lose his or her job for exposing the dysfunction, but once exposed, it's more likely to be healed.

Cultural Changes Affect the Church

Analysts seem to agree that we are in a period of significant change. Some claim that there has been more change in our world in the twentieth century than in the previous nineteen centuries combined, and that more changes occurred in the last decade of the twentieth century than in the first ninety years of the twentieth century.

When the calendar turned to 1000 a millennium ago, the world population was about 275 million. Now it's about 6 billion.

In 1900 a majority of Americans were employed in agriculture and the number two profession was "domestic servant." At the end of the century less than 2 percent of Americans work in agriculture and most Americans have never met a domestic servant.

Twenty percent of the member states of the United Nations were not countries in 1990.

The list of changes is very long and impressive. We live longer. We travel faster. We marry less and divorce more. We have smaller wars instead of bigger wars. We have many more college graduates. We work more and sleep less. We owe a lot more money. We have more women working outside the home than ever before.

The greatest changes have been technological. Fewer workers produce more products because of technology. Massive amounts of information are available to anyone who has access to the Internet or a library. CT scans and MRIs allow physicians to look inside our bodies without opening them up. Devastating diseases like smallpox and polio have been eradicated from our list of worries.

The church is not an isolated island but part of the world of change.[5]

There may not be a church building in North America without electricity. Most have telephones. A high number use overhead projectors, public address systems, video projectors, telephone answering machines, fax machines, and computers with e-mail, desktop publishing, word processing, and sophisticated databases.

Churches are also affected by the distinguishing characteristics of different generations (Builders, Boomers, Gen X, Millennials), the new role of women in society, the increase of families with everyone over fourteen working one or more jobs, decreased giving to charity, the shift from modern to postmodern thinking, and the ever changing styles of music.

Leadership is different in periods of change. The leader must simultaneously deal with followers who are destabilized by change and resistant to it and followers who are energized by change and eager for it. Many churches have both kinds of people.

One well-known critic of contemporary church music labeled it Seven-Eleven music—seven words repeated eleven times. A quick-witted responder said, "Oh, you mean music written by Handel." It's true that the "Hallelujah Chorus" from *Messiah* and other classical pieces have much repetition. The point is that the same churches have resisters and advocates.

This is further compounded by the lowered walls of denominationalism. In a sense, denominations were America's first franchisers. Whether you were Catholic, Lutheran, Presbyterian, or Methodist, you could go to another church of your denomination anywhere in the country and experience pretty much the same thing—identical liturgy, same Sunday school curriculum, denominational hymnal, and very similar beliefs. Today there are far greater variations within denominations, and many churches have people from a broad mix of denominational backgrounds.

The changes are so many that few leaders can keep up. It is embarrassing when you have a good education, read books and magazines, and try your best to know what is going on, and a friend at church talks to you about a new social trend you've never heard of. Even if the leader does "keep up," who has the wisdom to make good judgments on every issue? One social commentator claimed that human knowledge doubles every two years. If that's accurate, half of all human knowledge has come in the past twenty-four months. No one can keep up. Yet the information the leader does not know can have enormous importance to the church or other organizations being led.

Leadership Is Situational

Every context is different. Like a physician with a patient, each leader must study and diagnose before prescribing. What works in one place may be the worst possible approach in another place.

The complexity of the leadership task is enormous. Every church, community, and organization is different from the next. That is why some highly effective leaders fail miserably when they relocate. They try to repeat their successes, only to discover that their methods don't transcend time and place.

My father was an effective and successful pastor of the same church outside of New York City for thirty-three years. In many ways he was a brilliant and visionary leader with innovations ahead of his time. The church grew to a thousand members long before the era of megachurches. It was a multiple staff church in a time when even the largest congregations had a single pastor. The church made pioneering innovations in evangelism, education, music, radio, missions, and more. After retirement he served briefly as pastor of a church in south Florida. It was a difficult and disappointing experience. Although I never heard him say so, I think he thought he could repeat his success. He imagined that the style and ideas of the former church would work equally well in the new church. Success never returned. His style worked very well in New Jersey from the 1930s to the 1970s but not in Florida in the 1980s.

What was different? Frankly, it's hard to say. Sometimes the most careful study and analysis fails to reveal why the same leader does well in one situation and poorly in another. There are thousands of variables. Most of us cannot list, much less explain, all the variables, so we choose a few to blame or to explain. The truth is, the situational nature of leadership adds exponentially to the complexity of the task. No leader may ever assume that what works well in one place will work well in another. If Martin Luther and Martin Luther King Jr. had traded places in history, we probably never would have heard of either of them. They were the right leaders in the right places at the right times.

This also means that there are good and godly leaders who struggle and feel like failures when the results are no fault of their own. Probably the best leaders in the world wouldn't do any better there.

Trust and Respect Are More Difficult to Earn

The etymology of the old clergy title "parson" indicates that it came from a mispronunciation or colloquialism of the word "person." In today's slang, we would say, "He is the man!" (meaning "the most important guy around"). Generations ago the local minister was the most educated and well-traveled *person* in the community. He not only knew God and the Bible but he usually knew more about most things than most people did. Respect and trust came with the title.

Research by George H. Gallup Jr. shows that ministers are still among the most highly respected people in modern American culture.[6] But it's not like it used to be. The last half of the twentieth century has been a strange mix of high expectations and low trust for leaders.

People sense the need for highly capable and trustworthy leaders to navigate the waters of change—leaders who are intelligent, informed, wise, articulate, popular, visionary, unselfish, and highly ethical. Yet many leaders have been disappointing. Political and religious leaders have been exposed for unethical, unwise, immoral, and extremely selfish behavior.

Unfortunately, the failures of the few have undercut the many. Whether we like it or not, there is a widespread distrust of leaders, which makes the leadership task far more difficult. Skeptics think, "the only person I can really trust is myself."

Fortunately, leaders who are close to us are more trusted than leaders who are out of reach. This generally favors local churches and charities. People are willing to trust those they can see and doubt those who are far away and less accountable.

The head of a major religious publishing company claims he has a sign on his desk that says, "The old way: If you publish it, they will buy it; the new way: If you publish it, they will doubt it." In other words, trust must be earned, not assumed.

To earn trust takes a lot of time and effort. Leaders who are new and who have short tenure are significantly handicapped by the lack of automatic trust and respect.

Personal Problems

Not all difficulties are external to leaders. Many problems originate with the leaders themselves. Or at least the leaders' personal issues interact with the leadership context in such a way that the mix is disastrous.

The head of one Christian organization was charming on the platform and creative in programming, but argumentative and combative with members of the board of directors. His leadership style alienated him from board members and led first to institutional gridlock and then to involuntary termination. When he accepted a similar job in a comparable organization a few hundred miles away, the same script played out in almost the same way. From his perspective, religious organizations are difficult to lead and board members are all obstinate enemies. He doesn't consider that he could be the problem.

Two thousand miles away another leader works on a large staff as an associate rather than chief executive officer. He easily gets hired for good jobs, lasts only a few years, and keeps moving on. He "kisses up and kicks down" the organizational hierarchy. His superiors think highly of him, at least at first. But he berates and demeans volunteers and staff who report to him. In a tight situation he will promise anything, even if he knows he can't keep the promise. His subordinates soon distrust him and eventually quit. Without staff, he is unable to do his job, so he quits and moves on.

One old adage says that we tend to parent as we were parented. The corollary is that we tend to lead as we have been led. In each of these cases the leaders are following a style learned from parents and other leaders. It seemed to work for them. They are either so sure of its effectiveness or so ignorant of other possibilities that they continue to repeat patterns of failure.

Leaders have personal problems just like everyone else. John Wesley and Abraham Lincoln had difficult wives. Harry Truman's wife, Bess, didn't like living in Washington and spent much of her husband's presidency back in Independence, Missouri. Jonathan Edwards[7] was fired from his pastorate. Charles Haddon Spurgeon[8] suffered from painful gout and was overweight. Franklin Delano Roosevelt was disabled by polio but kept his disability a secret from the nation. Billy Graham preached to millions when his son Franklin was a prodigal. Nelson Mandela helped save South Africa from apartheid but couldn't save his own marriage from divorce. All of these are well-known "successful" leaders who lived with their problems and left their marks for good. Not everyone does so well. Some highly capable and deeply dedicated leaders are sabotaged by their personal issues. But the point is, leaders are not exempt from the greatest of human struggles, and those struggles add to the difficulty of leadership. It is hard to effectively lead the morning after a sleepless night caused by physical pain, marital discord, a prodigal son or daughter, financial struggles, or any of the other problems common to human experience.

Some people come to leadership positions who are themselves dysfunctional and thus impose their dysfunction on those they lead. Other leaders are simply in over their heads. They have been hired or elected to do what they are ill-equipped or unable to do. A friend of mine inherited the family business when his father suddenly died. His father was an outgoing, highly skilled entrepreneur with natural gifts and acquired leadership skills. His son is the opposite, with one exception. The son is wise. After a short time he realized that he was not suited to be president of the company, so he stepped aside and took a comparatively low-paying job as an employee in the company his father founded. As a result, the company has flourished, and the son is happy and highly respected.

Too Tough?

Why would anyone want to be a leader? Researcher George Barna reports that only 5 percent of American pastors claim to have the spiritual gift of leadership.[9] Thousands of church leaders wonder why they ever accepted leadership responsibilities, and many quit. They conclude that the job is too hard, the rewards are too few, and their abilities and gifts aren't right. Discouragement and defeat are epidemic.

As if this news isn't bad enough, potential future leaders are opting out before they get started. Many of the brightest and best choose other professions. Churches have trouble recruiting volunteers for leadership positions. People say, "I might be willing to serve on the committee but someone else will have to be chair."

My response: Of course leadership is hard. *Life* is hard! Anything worth accomplishing is hard. It is hard to be a good spouse, parent, neighbor, or friend. It is hard to get in good physical shape and maintain proper weight, cholesterol, and blood pressure. It is hard to get out of debt and to save money.

Moses didn't want to lead because he had a speech impediment. Saul hid when God wanted to anoint him king of Israel. Jonah was swallowed by a huge fish when he ran from the difficulties of leadership. Peter denied Jesus. Thomas doubted his resurrection. Even Jesus asked to be relieved of duty. "My Father, if it is possible, may this cup be taken from me" (Matthew 26:39).

As a pastor and church leader, I know that leadership is hard. I remember many of the times I wanted to quit. I often feel overwhelmed and underqualified. I know what it is like to preach on Sunday morning after a sleepless Saturday night with a sick child or other family issue. Yet it is not the difficulty or ease that makes a job worth doing. It is not even the successes or failures that are the ultimate measure of meaning. Leadership is doing what needs to be done. There can be great satisfaction in knowing what God has asked you to do and then doing it.

Chapter 3

Leadership Myths

Discouraged leaders are easy to find.
Leaders ready to quit are easy to find.
Look in almost any church.

One analyst gives the impression that all religious leaders are incompetent jerks. Another argues that most people in leadership positions aren't gifted to be leaders and should do something else with their lives. When these critics are heard and read by religious leaders, they think they may as well quit before they get fired.

Too many buy into mistaken leadership myths like these. The myths have many plots and subplots, but they all swirl around a common theme: *Leadership is all about the leader, and the leader must have all the right qualifications.*

Myth #1: Leaders must have all the right traits.

One of the methods we used to change and shape the direction of Wooddale Church was a series of leadership classes. Austin Chapman, then chairman of the church board, and I put together a simple six-week course called "Leaders' Forum," which consisted of ninety-minute sessions on six Wednesday evenings, a Saturday morning class of three hours, and a Sunday evening social gathering in one of our homes. The Leaders' Forum was by invitation only; we never announced it to the congregation or published it in the church bulletin. We invited twelve people, a mix of men and women, to attend the class. They were charged twenty-five dollars and were required to read books, write papers, and take tests. When the six weeks were over, we started over with twelve different people. We taught the classes every six weeks for two and one-half years. They became a catalyst for getting church leaders to agree on both the essential and massive changes needed to redirect the church.

During one of the first classes we asked group members to list the traits of a leader. They quickly came up with these: loving, kind, visionary, thoughtful, intelligent, articulate, courageous, godly, persuasive, wise, experienced, loyal, forgiving, hardworking, disciplined, prayerful.

Next we asked them to list the most famous leaders in history. Again, the answers were many and varied: Moses, David, Nehemiah, Julius Caesar, Aristotle, Genghis Khan, George Washington, Madame Curie, Adolph Hitler, Abraham Lincoln, Susan B. Anthony, Napoleon Bonaparte, George Washington Carver, Franklin Delano Roosevelt, Joan of Arc, John F. Kennedy, Idi Amin, Louis Pasteur, Nelson Mandela, Attila the Hun.

Then we asked, "Were all these leaders?"

"Yes."

"Did they have the traits previously listed?"

"No." Some had many. Some had a few. Some had almost none.

The truth is, there is no definitive list of leadership traits. As hard as many have tried, and despite all the books that have been written, there simply is no such list. Exceptions abound. Look at some examples of traits and exceptions:

Trait	Exception
Articulate	Moses had a speech impediment.
Desire to lead	Moses preferred to decline. Jonah ran away.
Moral	David was an adulterer and a murderer.
Wise	Solomon corrupted Israel with foreign wives and gods.
Relational	Paul couldn't get along with Barnabas (and others).
Visionary	Christopher Columbus didn't know where he was going and didn't know where he was when he got there.
Tolerant	Martin Luther was intolerant of peasants (and others).
Able to incite loyalty	Abraham Lincoln carried a minority of the popular vote.
Kindness	Adolf Hitler and Idi Amin were leaders who were ruthless.
Hard-working	President Eisenhower played a lot of golf; President Kennedy took afternoon naps.

These and other good traits certainly enhance the quality of leadership. In fact, the absence of good traits usually makes leadership less likely and more difficult. The point is that traits are *related* to leadership and *helpful* to leadership but not *essential* to leadership.

Serious students of leadership abandoned the trait theory in 1948 when Ralph Stogdill published his article "Personal Factors Associated With Leadership: A Survey of the Literature."[1] Professor J. Robert Clinton summarized Stogdill's writing in these words:

> Stogdill showed that leadership research from 1904 until 1948, which concentrated on the identification of traits of leaders, had proved inconclusive. The hope had

been that identification of traits of leaders would lead in turn to the early prediction of leaders who had these traits in embryonic form. Researchers, using empirical research techniques, sought to identify traits of leaders. They finally concluded that the study of traits of a leader apart from a leadership situation and followers was not adequate. Traits of leaders depended on contextual situations and followers as well as physical and cultural heritage. . . .

Stogdill suggested that certain situations and certain people require certain types of leaders. Therefore, a person who seems like a "born leader" in one setting, may be ineffective in another.

Though *potential* leaders are born, *effective* leaders are made as a result of 1. opportunity, 2. development, and 3. experience. Again, these three components do not guarantee that a person will rise to become a great leader. But without them it is unlikely that the person will realize his or her potential.[2]

Denominations and Christian organizations that put too much stock in predicting future leadership success based upon traits and test scores are making a mistake. Clinton says:

Some present-day Christian parachurch organizations and some denominations are seeking to identify traits of pastors, or church planters, or successful missionaries. The intent of these efforts is to recruit the right kind of people for these important tasks. Yet history is repeating itself. For the most part these efforts concentrate on the leaders alone just as was the case in the Early Trait Era (1904–1948). They do not analyze the dynamics of situations and followers in which they operate.[3]

Bottom line: Having certain traits doesn't guarantee effective leadership any more than lacking certain traits guarantees ineffective leadership. What the leader does with those traits is what matters most.

Myth #2: Leadership is all about leaders.

Jonathan Edwards may be America's greatest native-born thinker. He was a brilliant philosopher, theologian, writer, preacher, and educator. Although he is most famous for his sermon "Sinners in the Hands of an Angry God," we do him a disservice when we reduce his life and career to this single event. Many church historians of the eighteenth century agree that the Great Awakening, which brought spiritual revival to New England, began in Edwards' Northampton, Massachusetts, pulpit. Edwards read his sermons, rarely looking up. Those who value note-free speaking and constant audience eye contact would consider him a poor example of effective communication. But the spiritual response to his sermons and the resulting transformation of lives was nothing short of supernatural.

Yet Pastor Edwards was voted out of his church. By modern standards, this bad mark on his ministerial résumé meant he was a failure. He changed careers and became an itinerant missionary to Native Americans. Then, adding to the surprises of this amazing man, he was summoned to the presidency of the College of New Jersey (later named Princeton University). During his short tenure as university president he volunteered for a new medical procedure called smallpox vaccination. He wanted to set an example so others would take the vaccination and be spared from the deadly scourge of smallpox. It was a bold risk, and it cost him his life. Edwards contracted the disease and died.

Here's the question: Was Jonathan Edwards a good leader?

In terms of church polity, he was definitely a poor leader. He couldn't even convince his own congregation to retain him as their pastor. However, if measured by courage, example, spirituality, and impact on future generations, he may be judged as one of the greatest leaders in the history of the United States of America.

What would make a man so successful in one arena and so unsuccessful in another? While some will try to explain this in terms of the man alone, we must realize that leadership is far more complex than a single person. There are multiple variables. Every situation is different. In other words, it takes more than a leader to make leadership work.

I am privileged to pastor a church in Eden Prairie, Minnesota, where the congregation expects its leaders to succeed and is surprised if they fail. I hear of other churches, however, that expect their leaders to fail and are surprised if they succeed. To a significant degree, the leadership success I have enjoyed at Wooddale Church is more about the church than about me. For reasons I cannot explain, this is a church that helps people lead. I am convinced that I could pastor another church with similar external characteristics and end up ousted like Edwards.

One congregation in Minnesota fired three pastors in a row. The people of the church think it is astonishing bad luck that they stumbled across a threefold succession of losers. My read is just the opposite: This sick church has damaged three pastors in less than ten years. If I were the bishop, I wouldn't allow another minister to serve that church until some very serious intervention, repentance, and correction has taken place.

E. J. Elliston explains that "leadership always has three basic requirements: a leader, follower(s), and a situation. These elements are as essential to leadership as oxygen, fuel, and heat are to fire. If any one is removed, leadership will disappear—the fire will go out."[4]

Leadership is about leaders, followers, organizations, circumstances, power, history, and more. It is the relationship of each to the other that makes the leadership matrix. This is why leadership is both a science and an art. Some aspects of leadership can be measured; others cannot. What works in one place doesn't work in another. What is effective in one church is a disaster in another. This is not to say that a leader cannot be successful in two different places. Many leadership traits are transferable. An effective leader at one time and place may also be an effective leader at another time and place if other factors are present to fuel his leadership success.

Long and dangerous rivers like the Mississippi and the Amazon require both captains and pilots to navigate boats through the myriad of dangers. The captain is in charge of the boat from start to finish. However, a series of pilots board the vessel and take the wheel for especially treacherous stretches. One pilot may be a specialist for only a few miles of the river. He is responsible for knowing the location of every rock, sandbar, and current. He is paid to get the boat through that single stretch of the river. Along another stretch, a different pilot is needed who knows that particular area. But let's suppose that the pilot for miles 222–245 is transferred to the section covering miles 487– 498. The combination of his natural gifts, acquired skills, experience, and efforts to learn will probably enable him to be just as good downriver as he was upriver. It's not guaranteed, but the chances are good. The same is true of leaders. Those who succeed at one place and time may succeed at another place and time, but there are no guarantees. Clinton says, "Effective leaders maintain a learning posture throughout their lifetimes."[5]

Myth #3: All leaders are heroes.

"Where are today's leaders? Never have we needed so many and had so few." It's a common complaint; perhaps it always has been. All the great leaders seem to have lived in a different generation. Or perhaps the current generation seldom recognizes or appreciates the greatness of their leaders. Abraham Lincoln is repeatedly counted as one of history's great leaders, yet he was severely criticized during his presidency, and many did not grieve his assassination. Winston Churchill is renowned as the leader who saved Britain from defeat in World War II, yet he led his party to electoral defeat in 1945. In Churchill's case, he continued to be a hero but was no longer their chosen leader.

The cry for leaders is often the cry for heroes. While it is wonderful to have hero leaders, they are rare. Heroism is often the consequence of circumstances and opportunity, whereas leadership is a function of behavior. We want heroes because they are easy to idealize. Their followers often mimic their clothes, speech, beliefs, values, and even mannerisms. Heroes are "bigger than life" and become legends. They are quoted as if their words were inspired. When they leave, they are deeply grieved and long remembered.

Although World War II army general George S. Patton Jr. actually set out to become a hero as a method of leadership,[6] this approach doesn't usually work. Hero classification usually comes from a single act of unusual courage that becomes well known or from the selective adulation of someone with influence, often a biographer. Not all heroes are leaders. Sometimes they almost trip into their status of heroism like Forrest Gump in the classic movie starring Tom Hanks.

The truth is, very few leaders are heroes. Most leaders never risk their lives in battle or distinguish themselves by their courage. Most leaders work quietly, and their effectiveness comes as a result of a long series of wise decisions and good behavior. Most leaders are known in a very limited sphere.

Just as leadership and heroism rarely combine, leadership and celebrity rarely mix well. This is especially true for Christians. There could be a theological debate as to the appropriateness of Christians becoming celebrities. The notoriety and perquisites often destroy those who do. Celebrity is not the same as fame. To be famous is to be well known. To be a celebrity is to have a status above others, to be elevated and honored in ways not available to almost everyone else. The danger with celebrity is that it so often causes a person to think more highly of himself than he ought to think.[7]

The myth is that true leaders are also heroes and celebrities. The truth is that most effective leaders are little known and seldom honored outside of the community where they live or the ministry they serve. Leaders are otherwise ordinary people who do what needs to be done in the time and place where God has put them.

Myth #4: Pastors must have the gift of leadership.

Most pastors admit they don't have the spiritual gift of leadership. Many feel so pressured to have it that they think they'll be asked to resign if they don't fake having it.

Romans 12:4–8 contains the only biblical mention of the gift of leadership:

> Just as each of us has one body with many members, and these members do not all have the same function, so in Christ we who are many form one body, and each member belongs to all the others. We have different gifts, according to the grace given us. If a man's gift is prophesying, let him use it in proportion to his faith. If it is serving, let him serve; if it is teaching, let him teach; if it is encouraging, let him encourage; if it is contributing to the needs of others, let him give generously; if it is *leadership*, let him govern dili-

gently; if it is showing mercy, let him do it cheerfully.

Several observations are critical:

- Leadership is only one gift among many and is not a "greater gift" (Romans 12:31).
- Spiritual gifts are primarily given to the church, not to the individual.
- The emphasis in Romans 12 is not on *having* the gift but on leading or governing "diligently."

The practical conclusion is that the person in a leadership role should be diligent and coordinate with the rest of the body in being and doing what the body (church) is supposed to do. It is not some magical dust that falls on one person to make her or him a hero or a celebrity. Leadership is about getting a job done.

Leaders "Do"

If all these are myths about leadership, does this mean that qualifications don't matter? Of course not. Qualifications for leadership are very important. After all, the New Testament itself spells out the qualifications for church leaders:

> Here is a trustworthy saying: If anyone sets his heart on being an overseer, he desires a noble task. Now the overseer must be above reproach, the husband of but one wife, temperate, self-controlled, respectable, hospitable, able to teach, not given to drunkenness, not violent but gentle, not quarrelsome, not a lover of money. He must manage his own family well and see that his children obey him with proper respect. (If anyone does not know how to manage his own family, how can he take care of God's church?) He must not be a recent convert, or he may become conceited and fall under the same judgment as the devil. He must also have a good reputation with outsiders, so that he will not fall into disgrace and into the devil's trap. (1 Timothy 3:1–7)

Qualifications, yes, but qualifications based on actions. When this person could have lost his temper, he was self-controlled. When he could have gotten drunk, he stayed sober. When he could have picked a quarrel, he worked for peace and harmony. Conclusion? He is qualified to lead the church. Church leadership is based on what a person has done in the past.

Consider the prospectus of any mutual fund. There are tables and narratives explaining the return on investment over the past one, three, five, and ten years. Then there is usually a statement that says, "Past performance does not guarantee future return." That's more than a statement for legal protection; it's a statement about the way life works. Past performance does not guarantee future behavior, but it is the best indicator we have. Few investors would invest ten thousand dollars in a mutual fund that had lost 50 percent of its money for each of the past ten years. Performance is not the only indicator, but it is usually the best indicator of how a mutual fund (or a person) will behave in the future. Paul applies this concept to the selection of leaders in the New Testament church when he recommends that they review past performance before selecting future church leaders.

The modern study of leadership has thousands of books that can be grouped into seven general views of leadership: trait, situational, organizational, power, vision, ethics, and authenticity. Each has some validity. Most of us can probably learn and grow from the teachings and writings of each perspective. However, it all eventually comes down to what a person does.

Leadership is what we do.

The previous one-sentence paragraph will elicit from some this reaction: "What we do is based on who we are. Character determines behavior." Of course it does, but to paraphrase James 2:18, "Show me your character without deeds, and I will show you my character by what I do."

Many people have wonderful character but poor leadership skills. It is just as possible to have great character and be a poor leader as it is to be a strong leader and have lousy character. Although it's not right to wrongly lead, it's often done. The correct and Christian approach is to combine character and leadership and thereby to lead Christianly.

So how is this lived out in the life of a church or other Christian organization? Should the person in leadership focus on being or doing? The answer is both; the two are integrally connected. Learn from others. Grow spiritually. Use your gifts. Be the best you can be. But don't get hung up on missing traits, a quest for greatness, worry about having or not having the gift of leadership, or assuming that you are totally responsible. The primary leadership questions are:

- What is my leadership mission?[8]
- What do I need to do in order to help achieve the mission?

About a year after graduating from seminary I concluded that the church I served wasn't evangelistic and that evangelism was central to the mission of the church. My intuitive solution was to preach a series of sermons telling the congregation to reach out to others and be evangelistic. It was an exercise in both hypocrisy and ineffectiveness. I was not myself evangelistic, and the sermon series made no apparent difference in the church. The series did make me feel better, though, because it moved guilt off my shoulders and onto the people of the church.

As a leader, I needed to do more than talk about evangelism. That would not be easy for me because I do not have the gift of evangelism. Up to that point in my life I had led only one person to Christian faith (at a camp where I was a counselor, a camper more or less forced me to explain the Gospel). Neither my seminary degree nor my Certificate of Ordination meant much when it came to actual evangelism.

Then I stumbled across Paul's advice to Timothy to "keep your head in all situations, endure hardship, do the work of an evangelist, discharge all the duties of your ministry" (2 Timothy 4:5).

It seemed quite practical to tell a young church leader to keep his head when facing the challenges of pastoral ministry. It was encouraging to know that Christian leaders have always faced hardship and need to persevere. It was a good reminder to faithfully discharge the wide array of ministry responsibilities. But mixed in with all this general advice was the direct admonition to "do the work of an evangelist." Apparently Timothy pastored a church that needed to learn how to reach out to unchurched unbelievers. He faced what I was facing.

Timothy needed to get going and just do it—do what an evangelist does. What I found most impressive, but also most troubling, was the lack of any evidence that Timothy had the gift of evangelism (Ephesians 4:11). In other words, it was Timothy's role as a leader that called him to do evangelism, not his ability, experience, or giftedness.

About this time a friend introduced me to the book and method called *Evangelism Explosion*.[9] I read and reread the volume and practiced the approach. Then, following the advice of the book, I took a layman from the congregation along with me on a visit to a stranger's home to try evangelizing. It was a disaster. The visit did not go well. I think I embarrassed them, and I know I embarrassed myself. I learned a powerful and practical principle that I wish had been written in the book: When you are going to make a fool of yourself, go alone!

The following month I devoted two evenings each week to visiting several homes. The people I visited had either come to the church or were new to the community. Some of my worst fears were realized, including rejection and anger. But for the most part people were amazingly receptive and gracious. For the first time in my life I had many meaningful conversations about the Christian faith with people who were not yet committed believers. After weeks of knocking on doors, sitting in living rooms, and carrying on conversations, a couple indicated that they wanted to believe. I helped them understand the Gospel and what it meant to become a disciple of Jesus Christ. They came to the church, were baptized, made friends, grew spiritually, and became involved. After a few more successes, I again tried taking observers along. Months later I began taking a couple of people with me every Tuesday and Thursday evening. The numbers grew until more than a hundred people were trained in evangelism. The impact on the church was significant and encouraging. Growth came through outreach. The mission of the church was being accomplished.[10]

Did I feel more comfortable? Did I receive the gift of evangelism? Was this something I chose to continue doing? No, on all counts. Others took over and I moved on to other things. Support became sufficient without personal direct leadership. I had done what 2 Timothy 4:5 advised another young pastor to do—"the work of an evangelist."

For others in leadership positions, the task to be accomplished may be to clarify the church's vision, to raise funds, to confront someone whose temper is out of control, to disciple, to reorganize, to develop a new approach to music, to teach Christian doctrine, to pray, or any of a thousand other tasks that churches and Christian organizations need to do in order to fulfill their mission. The leader steps up and does what needs to be done.

Leadership is figuring out what needs to be done and then doing it.

Chapter 4

Complexity—Nothing Seems Simple Anymore

TWO REFORMED CHURCHES were founded the same year in the same New Jersey town. One is flourishing and the other is failing. Calvary Reformed Church boasts 275 families, a large budget, and a strong parochial school. First Reformed Church is down to fewer than 40 families, hasn't met the decreasing budget once in the past ten years, and closed its school nine years ago.

It could be a difference in pastors, but both churches have changed pastors twice in the past decade. The style of music is pretty much the same. Location, of course, is different, but not different enough to explain why one is flourishing and the other is floundering. The people at Calvary Reformed Church seem friendlier, but the people at First Reformed Church seem to pray more. Does this mean that friendliness is more important than prayer?

Compare the merger of two independent missions organizations. Both call themselves "faith" missions, originally meaning that their missionaries trusted God and donors rather than a denominational budget for financial support. Both missions began in the post–World War II period of evangelical entrepreneurship. Both were founded by charismatic leaders who had great vision for evangelizing Asians and Africans. Both subsequently expanded to send missionaries to Latin America and Europe, especially Eastern Europe after 1991. One grew. One shrank. They merged and the new united mission shrank. Board meetings and executive staff retreats have been consumed with finding the answer. The assumption has been that something is wrong; they need to figure out what is wrong and fix it, and then everything will be all right again. Maybe it's not that simple. In fact, maybe nothing is wrong; maybe it's just that the original goals don't fit the new century as well as they did the old one. Maybe the organizations served a generation that is retiring and dying and therefore has no future. Maybe there should be another merger because it is easier to create a new corporate culture out of a three-way merger than to merge two existing cultures into one. Maybe the leadership has diverted all of its energy into figuring out what is wrong instead of focusing on and fulfilling the purpose of the organization. Maybe . . . maybe . . . maybe.

The twenty-first century will be complex. Simple answers will be hard to find if they even exist.

Multiple Variables

I define complexity as *having multiple variables.* Think of the room in which you are reading this book. Whether or not you are comfortable depends on multiple variables: temperature, humidity, amount of light, air movement, presence or absence of other people, noise, size and design of your chair, how much sleep you had last night, what you ate for your last meal, the state of your health, and whether you find this book interesting or boring. It would be simplistic for me to claim that your comfort depends on room temperature alone. Raising or lowering the temperature may or may not make any difference. In some cases, a little more heat would make you comfortable. In others, raising the temperature would only make you realize how uncomfortable your chair is. All of these interconnecting variables determine your level of comfort. Complexity is the presence and interrelationship of all these variables.

So what's new? Some analysts argue that the basics of life aren't any different today than they were a hundred or a thousand years ago. We all deal with the issues of survival, relationships, meaning, and destiny, no matter where our generation falls on the calendar of history. To some extent, that is true. However, the twenty-first century is a chapter of history with more variables than any previous generation. Earlier generations could communicate verbally face-to-face, through a messenger, or in writing. Today's generation can communicate verbally face-to-face, by voice mail, by tape recording, by video recording, by telephone, by video teleconferencing, in writing via paper, e-mail, facsimile, or even the alphanumeric display on a pager. Multiple variables do not make life better or worse, but they do make it more complex. An earlier generation may have dealt with a thousand variables in a critical leadership decision, but today we're dealing with ten thousand.

Church people are not limited to other church members in their relationships and experiences. The complexity of society surrounds and penetrates the church and religious organizations. Divorce, remarriage, and blended families are one example. Regardless of a church's theology and practice regarding divorce and remarriage, few congregations remain unaffected by it. The increasing number of blended families and joint-custody situations means that children are with different parents in different locations on alternate weekends. This makes it impossible for a Sunday school teacher to assume children will have Sunday-to-Sunday continuity in their religious education. Each lesson must stand alone. In some cases children are being taught contradictory doctrines on alternate weekends. Adding to the challenge are families that are not blended and have their children in class every Sunday. They don't want the curriculum "watered down" to suit those who come only half the time. Indeed, these parents may demand continuity, high expectations, tests, and grades. Christian education leaders face these and other competing variables in our complex society.

The success or failure of a church may hinge on an almost unlimited combination of variables including doctrine, denomination, location, pastor, layleadership, style of music, racial and socioeconomic makeup, relevance of preaching, and spiritual receptivity of members. There are also more mundane variables including times of services, cultural relevance, financial resources, and the size of the parking lot.

Complexity is compounded by the increased heterogeneity of the general population and the church congregation. Most Sunday mornings I preach to an audience that may include lifelong Christians, visiting Muslims, newcomers who have never been to church before and have never read the Bible, retirees, newborns, millionaires, AFDC single mothers, major league athletes, terminal cancer patients, Calvinists, Arminians, Baptists, Lutherans, and Roman Catholics. I am forced to communicate differently than I would to a homogeneous audience in which everyone believed the same and looked alike.

If nothing else, complexity has reduced the power of church franchising in North America. There are so many combinations of people and communities that it is much more difficult to transfer what works well in one place and make it work in another.

Simple Solutions

In the midst of all this complexity, nothing is quite so attractive as a simple solution. There are legions of self-professed prophets who insist that they have *the* key that will unlock every complexity. They say: "pray more," "open the church to people with alternative lifestyles," "teach doctrine," "raise the standards," "discipline and exclude people with alternative lifestyles," "become all things to all people," "know who you are and stand for what you believe even if you stand alone," "pray for revival," "begin a men's ministry," "give altar calls," "require gender equity on the church board and church staff," "promote racial reconciliation," and the list goes on. Some proponents have programs for sale, others are single-theme consultants, and many sponsor church "how-to" conferences. Many of these are indeed wonderful things to do. Certainly no one should minimize the power and importance of prayer. However, the harsh reality is that the proponents of single solutions often leave a wake of disaster and disillusionment be-

hind them. Too many church leaders move from one inappropriately simple solution to the next. Many don't make any difference; some do lots of harm; a few are beneficial. North
Americans are prone to believe that a single pill can cure whatever is wrong. Real life is far more complex. While simple solutions work often enough to provide anecdotal evidence of effectiveness, they should not be the strategy of twenty-first
century leaders of the church of Jesus Christ.

Understanding Some of the Variables

To pretend that any list of variables is sufficient to inform
leaders of all they will deal with in the twenty-first century
would be simplistic. The purpose of examples is to help leaders
grapple with the concept of complexity. Once alerted to the
complexity of leadership issues, it then becomes critical to develop the skills of learning, analyzing, and prioritizing the many
variables.

Spiritual renewal

Some religious organizations and churches are spiritually
dying or dead. They may be Christian in name, history, mission
statement, board leadership, membership, and programming,
but they have no spiritual vitality. In some cases they have wan-
dered so far from the Christian faith that the founders wouldn't
recognize the organization. In other cases, they have focused so
intensely on all of the wrong things that they no longer know
what the right things are. These churches have no sense of the
presence and power of God; they no longer teach the Bible because they don't consider it to be supernatural; and while remaining technically orthodox, they've become spiritually
sterile. When the horse is dead, dismount.

If a church lacks God, it really isn't a church. Changing pastors, putting up a new sign, or offering appealing programs
won't do much good without spiritual renewal. In the words of
Psalm 127:1, "Unless the Lord builds the house, its builders
labor in vain." In some cases, the principle of unintended consequences may combine with complexity to bring unanticipated

results. A spiritually dead church, hoping to rebuild institution-ally, may call a new pastor and get a leader who is a catalyst for spiritual change they never planned. Often variables work in ways no one can plan or anticipate.

Several years ago the head of an American denomination told me the story of his long-established group of churches. They were in an obvious long-term slide toward fewer churches, fewer members, lower income, and sagging morale. The leadership hired a national consultant to study the denom-ination and make recommendations to stop the decline and bring renewal. After extensive study the consultant met with the denominational leaders. This is what he said: "From everything I have discovered, this denomination has fallen on such hard times that there is no reversal possible. In a few years you will be out of business. I have no recommendations that will help." Because it was almost lunchtime he suggested they adjourn the meeting and go eat. He started to walk out of the conference room, leaving a sobered group of leaders stuck in their chairs. One broke the silence: "Isn't there anything we can do?" The consultant replied, "The only thing I can think of is to get down on your knees and plead with God for mercy." (Not typical ad-vice from a consultant!) He left the room. More silence. One leader got up from his chair, turned around, and knelt to pray. Another did the same. One by one they all followed until every leader in the room was kneeling to pray. They missed lunch. The prayer meeting was spontaneous and supernatural. It lasted a long time.[1]

I heard this story three years after it happened. During that time the denomination experienced a spiritual renewal, its most productive period of new church starts in history, and was well on its way to doubling in size in less than ten years.

Without a doubt, I believe in spiritual renewal. But I must warn myself and others not to fall into the trap of making spir-itual renewal the simple catch-all solution to every complex problem churches and denominations face. It is possible for a spiritually renewed church to still have numerous unsolved problems. Take a look at what happened in the first-century Jerusalem church:

In those days when the number of disciples was increasing, the Grecian Jews among them complained against the Hebraic Jews because their widows were being overlooked in the daily distribution of food.

So the Twelve gathered all the disciples together and said, "It would not be right for us to neglect the ministry of the word of God in order to wait on tables. Brothers, choose seven men from among you who are known to be full of the Spirit and wisdom. We will turn this responsibility over to them and will give our attention to prayer and the ministry of the word."

This proposal pleased the whole group. They chose Stephen, a man full of faith and of the Holy Spirit; also Philip, Procorus, Nicanor, Timon, Parmenas, and Nicolas from Antioch, a convert to Judaism. They presented these men to the apostles, who prayed and laid their hands on them.

So the word of God spread. The number of disciples in Jerusalem increased rapidly, and a large number of priests became obedient to the faith. (Acts 6:1–7)

This must have been a significant crisis in the Jerusalem church for this story to be told in the book of Acts. Perhaps the future of the church was in jeopardy due to the risk of schism over ethnic rivalries. Wise leaders were aware of the importance of the ministry of the word, but they also recognized that inappropriate handling of money and ethnic differences could divide the whole church. So the apostles decided to put seven men in charge of the benevolence funds so prayer and ministry would not be neglected. The seven managers selected all had Greek names. In other words, they were chosen from the ethnic minority within the church that had complained about not getting their fair share of benevolence money. This was not a spiritual solution (there is no indication they even prayed about it). It was an organizational solution based on the recognition of human nature and relationships.

The apostles put first things first. Prayer and ministry of the word were more important than anything else. But they recognized the complexity of the situation and addressed each of the multiple variables that needed attention.

Some prophets will always insist that the leader's only responsibility is spiritual. I appreciate the emphasis but not the oversimplification. Prophets are difficult to argue against because they seem so spiritual. When practical solutions are suggested for churches and Christian organizations, the prophet says, "Those are human solutions, not spiritual solutions." The accusations roll out that church leaders are more managers than pastors, that marketing is a tool of the modern mind but not the Holy Writ, that we're meeting people's felt needs instead of obeying God's commandments. I've heard all of this many times and I am repeatedly saddened by the small view of God. Do we not believe that God can cure directly through a miracle or indirectly through a surgeon or prescription? Do we not acknowledge both divine sovereignty and human responsibility? Let our view of God be large enough to allow God to work through multiple means in addressing the multiple variables of leadership. Yes, the highest priority is spiritual, but it is not the only priority. Just as God is the God of all truth, God is the God of multiple means.

Theological and organizational perspectives

North Americans divide and subdivide into many different theological camps. In broad groupings there are liberals (e.g., Protestant Episcopal Church, Presbyterian Church U.S.A., United Church of Christ, etc.), moderates (American Baptists, United Methodists, Evangelical Lutheran Church in America, etc.), and conservatives (Southern Baptist Convention, Lutheran Church—Missouri Synod, Church of the Nazarene, etc.).[2] Which church or denomination a leader leads varies greatly by theological perspective. Even within denominations there are great variations between individual churches, as evidenced by the disagreements between moderate and conservative Southern Baptists, between the orthodox and liberal elements of the Episcopal Church, and among an extraordinary variety of theological extremes within American Baptist churches.

Add to the liberal-conservative continuum the different approaches taken in church government and the picture becomes even more complex. There are three basic forms of church government, each analogous to specific forms of secular government.

State/Leadership	Church/Leadership
Monarchy/King	Episcopal/Bishop
Republic/Representatives	Presbyterian/Elders
Democracy/People	Congregational/Members

The forms of church government are actually denominational names. It should be noted, however, that the largest group of people under an "episcopal" form of government is the world's one billion Roman Catholics. Also, denominations with a "presbyterian" form of government include such denominations as the Christian Reformed Church and the Reformed Church in America. The largest Protestant denomination in the United States is the Southern Baptist Convention, which is ruled by a "congregational" form of government.

Many of the adherents of these very different systems will forcefully argue that theirs is the biblical way. All have biblical backing, and the decision of which to follow grows out of each group's interpretation of the New Testament.

Adding to the complexity of leadership within church government is the variety of expressions of each. Large Baptist churches, which technically espouse congregational government, often are run by a very strong board that functions in a style that is more presbyterian than congregational. Some are run by senior ministers who have as much power as bishops in Catholic or Episcopal churches. Saying a church is "congregational" doesn't mean the members really run the church. At the other extreme are Roman Catholic churches that have parish councils that vote on important decisions. They have not abandoned church law, but they've been greatly influenced by the democratic sense of individualism that permeates North American society.

Christian organizations don't fit any of the three categories. Most parachurch organizations don't even pretend to follow a biblical model of government. They follow the American corporate model without apology. They are owned and governed by a board of directors, usually self-perpetuating, and not legally accountable to anyone outside of themselves. The top leader holds the office of president and is called the chief executive officer. There are vice-presidents, directors, managers, and associates. Yet despite their structural differences, many of these Christian organizations share the same values and goals as churches.

Leaders sometimes move from one type of organization to another, and foolish is the leader who discounts the organizational differences. In some organizations, change must first be approved by the bishop, in others, the board, in others, the members. In some, the president decides and that's it. Knowing which is which is more than an interesting piece of information; it's the difference between success and failure.

Size

The size of an organization is one of the most significant variables of all. Canadian sociologist Reginald W. Bibby conducted an extensive study of churches in the United States and Canada for the Protestant Church-owned Publishers Association and the Lilly Endowment. He found that while most churches are small, most people attend larger churches. Here are some interesting examples from Bibby's research:

- Almost 70 percent of all the people who attend services regularly are found in about 35 percent of churches, namely [churches of] 150 or more.[3]
- Megachurches with more than 1,000 active members and adherents comprise only 1 percent of all churches.[4]
- In general, the larger the church, the broader the range of its programs and activities.[5]
- As church size increases, so does congregational diversity with respect to characteristics such as age, marital status, and, to some extent, race. Such diversity results in the expansion of programs and activities and the need for more extensive resources. Increases in size are accompanied by an increase in the number of paid ministers and other staff. Leadership tends to lay in the hands of specialized ministerial personnel.[6]

As an organization increases in size, it also increases in complexity, because an increase in people means an increase in variables such as age, race, education, beliefs, socioeconomic status, and other factors. And as the complexity of the organization increases, so does the complexity of leadership that is needed.

Bibby uses the typology of Arlin Rothauge to categorize churches by size.[7] The Family Church has 50 or fewer people. The Pastoral Church has 50–150. The Program Church has 150–350. The Corporation Church has more than 350. He goes on to explain:

- *The Family Church*, whether new or old, possesses the dynamics of a family that follows the lead and temperament of a few "patriarchs and matriarchs."
- *The Pastoral Church* has an effective pastoral leader and strong family and friendship ties.
- *The Program Church* delegates more responsibility to the laity; social links are not as close.
- *The Corporation Church* is characterized by the importance of governing boards and the head pastor, and by greater program complexity and division of labor; social relations take the form of small groups.[8]

All of this has enormous significance for the twenty-first century leader. Large churches and organizations are more complex not only because they have more people but because they have more varieties of people. Greater complexity, however, does not necessarily mean greater difficulty. There are some Family Churches and Pastoral Churches that are notoriously difficult to lead. They have social structures based on longtime family relationships. The pastor may spend a lifetime in the church and the community and never be fully accepted because he has no blood relationship to other church members. The leader is expected to lead but forbidden to lead because the pastor is always an outsider. Also, there are some Corporation Churches that are comparatively easy to lead. They are well-organized, healthy institutions with clear divisions of labor. The senior pastor is expected to set the vision and preach the sermons. The staff and membership have a high level of respect for the senior pastor and are inclined to agree with and support the vision. Corporation Churches often have many competent leaders because the pool from which to draw is larger. So the correlation between size and difficulty to manage is not direct.

At the same time, do not underestimate the skills and work required to lead a highly complex organization.

Concepts for Leading in Complexity

The examples of complexity include much more than spiritual condition, theological and organizational perspectives, and size. Taking into account such factors as the leader's profile (age, education, experience, health, physical appearance, gender, etc.), the history of the church or organization (age, financial resources, decision-making patterns, facilities, etc.), and the community (village, town, suburb, city, state or province, nation, world), a church's profile could be as long as a small city's telephone book listing. What we need are some concepts for leading in complexity, especially twenty-first century complexity.

Acknowledge complexity

Successful leadership of complex organizations requires an acknowledgment and understanding of complexity. Some leaders grasp it intuitively. Others need to work at avoiding overly simple explanations, identifying the variables they must consider, weighing the effect of each variable on decisions, and managing each of the variables in ways that will fulfill the mission of the leader and the organization.

Those unwilling to deal with complexity should stay out of complex situations. On the other hand, leaders dare not discount simple solutions. This may sound contradictory, but actually it is not. For centuries physicians developed all types of treatment for diseases without realizing that the diseases were caused by bacteria they could not see. "Germ theory" was a simple answer to the complex problem of many dangerous illnesses. Many doctors were unwilling to accept such a simple solution as washing their hands before suturing a wound or delivering a baby. As basic as it now seems, hand washing by physicians had a profound and revolutionary effect on the practice of medicine. It was a simple solution to a complex problem. The same can happen in leadership situations. That said, the establishment of a sterile field for surgical procedures does not guarantee a cure for every malady. If anything, the understanding of germs and washing of hands and instruments has taken medicine to a new level of complexity that was previously unseen and unimaginable.

Consider the entire system

"Systems theory" has become increasingly well known to modern leaders. It is closely aligned with our understanding of complexity.

Interestingly, systems theory is not a new concept. In fact, it is intrinsic to the New Testament teachings about the church and spiritual gifts. Systems theory says that all parts of an organism or organization are interconnected and interrelated. When you change the whole, every part is affected. When you change any part, the whole is affected.

> The body is a unit, though it is made up of many parts; and though all its parts are many, they form one body. So it is with Christ. For we were all baptized by one Spirit into one body—whether Jews or Greeks, slave or free—and we were all given the one Spirit to drink.
>
> Now the body is not made up of one part but of many. If the foot should say, "Because I am not a hand, I do not belong to the body," it would not for that reason cease to be part of the body. And if the ear should say, "Because I am not an eye, I do not belong to the body," it would not for that reason cease to be part of the body. If the whole body were an eye, where would the sense of hearing be? If the whole body were an ear, where would the sense of smell be? But in fact God has arranged the parts in the body, every one of them, just as he wanted them to be. If they were all one part, where would the body be? As it is, there are many parts, but one body.
>
> The eye cannot say to the hand, "I don't need you!" And the head cannot say to the feet, "I don't need you!" On the contrary, those parts of the body that seem to be weaker are indispensable, and the parts that we think are

less honorable we treat with special honor. And the parts that are unpresentable are treated with special modesty, while our presentable parts need no special treatment. But God has combined the members of the body and has given greater honor to the parts that lacked it, so that there should be no division in the body, but that its parts should have equal concern for each other. If one part suffers, every part suffers with it; if one part is honored, every part rejoices with it.

Now you are the body of Christ, and each one of you is a part of it. (1 Corinthians 12:12–27)

The leader considers the impact of decisions and changes on the entire organization. Examples abound. Removing one problem board member will change the way the entire board functions and will affect the relationships of all the board members to each other. Adding an additional Sunday morning worship service will affect not only those who attend the new service but also those who continue to attend the old one. Adding a new degree program in a college or seminary will have ramifications for the students, faculty, and staff in all the existing programs.

The corollary says that to change the part, the whole must change. The classic example is an intervention in which many people in an alcoholic's system of relationships participate. For example, Curtis returns home from work one afternoon to find his wife, brother, best friend, pastor, boss, and parents waiting in his living room. The pastor graciously but firmly explains that they are all concerned about his drinking problem and want to help. A place has been reserved for him at a nearby residential treatment center. His bag is packed. The car is waiting to take him there immediately. His boss will protect his job and continue his paychecks. His wife will participate in the counseling. His parents will take care of the children. His best friend will stand by no matter what it takes. His pastor will pray and counsel and coordinate the whole process. But if Curtis refuses, he will probably face termination from his job, divorce from his wife, alienation from his friend, discipline by his church, and the disappointment of his parents. This strategy is based on the recognition that treatment alone is not enough. The support of his best friend is not enough. The threats of his wife are not enough. If Curtis is going to change, everyone in his system of relationships must cooperate.

The twenty-first century leader realizes that changing one important part of a ministry may require the involvement of the entire ministry. The support of all other leaders must be solicited. Seemingly distant and unrelated parts of the organization will have to do their part. Sacrifices will be required. Complexity and systems theory come together in all organizational changes. The leader is the manager of the process and the parts, determining what needs to be done and making sure that it is done.

Adopt a personal philosophy

"Keep an open mind!" is popular advice that can destroy a leader. If taken to an extreme, an open mind considers every fact, equally weighs every proposal, and never prejudges any situation. In the first place, this is impossible to do. No one can know all the options, and certainly no one can predict the results of every option. Even if it were possible, it would take too long. There is too much relevant information to consider for every decision. Some proposals from well-meaning church members aren't compatible with the purpose of the church or are not worth considering. To make the many decisions called for, the leader must exclude a majority of the alternatives or the decision will be made by inaction and default.

The better alternative is for every leader to adopt a personal philosophy, or theology, through which he or she will view all information. In other words, leaders must start with many presuppositions. The pastor cannot decide every Sunday between Calvinism, Arminianism, and Process Theology. The church cannot be led by episcopal polity in January, presbyterian polity in March, and congregational polity in November. The preacher cannot believe in miracles when preaching from the Old Testament but deny miracles when preaching from the New Testament. Instead, the effective third millennium leader will have a consistent and coherent theological system and management approach. This approach will provide a basis for filtering and processing information, build a platform for making critical decisions, save huge amounts of time, and provide consistent and predictable leadership.

Try answering the following questions:

- What is your theological system?
- What is your philosophy of leadership?
- What are your primary goals?
- What are you unwilling to do?

Some answers will be long and complex. Others will be quick and simple. But if you have no idea how to answer these four questions, leadership will be a painful and arduous process.

Does this mean that leaders can never change? No, leaders can and do change. But some important advice is in order.

- *Fundamental changes in leaders are potentially destabilizing to organizations and to the people they lead.* Changes in leaders have an impact far greater than changes in others and may be greater than bringing in a completely new leader.
- *Don't change too often.* Switching from Calvinist to Arminian theology, or from a highly directive to a nondirective leadership style, will profoundly affect all those who are led. But to change back and forth or to keep changing will probably alienate the leader's constituency and potentially destroy the organization.
- *Give followers time to catch up.* The leader may have fully processed his new approach, but an announcement does not bring followers up to speed on the same day. They need to listen, learn, process, and finally accept or reject.

Terry and Debbie Hollister pastored a Baptist General Conference Church in Billings, Montana. The Hollisters and the church changed both theology and denomination to affiliate with the new denomination of the Association of Vineyard Churches. The theology moved from noncharismatic to charismatic. The polity moved from congregational to episcopal. The church's affiliation and their ministerial credentials changed from a denomination more than a century old with deep Swedish immigrant roots to a recent denomination born in southern California. On one hand, the change was not totally radical, in that both denominations and traditions are part of American evangelicalism. On the other hand, this was a pretty big relocation within evangelicalism. It was not a hasty change, however. The Hollisters and the church talked and prayed and sought the counsel of many outside their local congregation. Everything possible was done to maintain and enhance positive relationships with both denominations. When the church made its official switch, leaders from both denominations were present to give their blessing.

This is a good example of adopting a clear and systematic approach to both theology and leadership. It is also an example of making significant change. It worked once. It probably shouldn't be done again, at least not for a very long time. Twenty-first century leaders need to know where they are going, have a philosophy for managing the journey, and stick with that philosophy for the long haul.

Complexity

One futurist claimed that at the turn of the millennium, human knowledge will be doubling every seventeen days. I question how anyone could be sure of such a statistic. (A friend of mine has a T-shirt that says, "87 percent of statistics are made up on the spur of the moment.") But let's give him the benefit of the doubt and say that the statistic is correct. If he means that information available to humans doubles every seventeen days, we are in a sea of data. There is more information on almost any subject than any person can process in a lifetime. This adds more and more alternatives. It multiplies alternatives. It is complexity squared. Life and leadership will become more and more complex as we move further into the twenty-first century.

Chapter 5

Busyness—There's Never Enough Time

TIME HASN'T CHANGED. There are still 24 hours every day, 168 hours every week, and 8,760 hours every year. The numbers were the same a generation ago, a century ago, a millennium ago. And the numbers for the twenty-first century will be the same as thcy were for the twentieth. But the way people use those hours is significantly altering the way we lead the church.

Working More

In 1997 the typical full-time[1] American employee worked 47.1 hours each week, compared to 43.6 hours per week in 1977.[2]

That is a far cry from the predictions of 1960s futurists who said the major industry of the country would become leisure due to ever-shortening workweeks. Consider the changes over twenty years:[3]

	1977	1997
Married employees with spouses also employed	66%	78%
Married male employees with employed spouses and children under 18	49%	67%
Percent of workers who bring home work at least once a week	23%	33%
Time that employed, married fathers spend with children per day	1.8 hours	2.3 hours
Time that employed, married mothers spend with children per day	3.3 hours	3.0 hours
Time married men employees spend on personal activities per workday	2.2 hours	1.6 hours
Time married women employees spend on personal activities per workday	1.7 hours	1.3 hours

These statistics are based on the "National Study of the Changing Workforce" conducted by Lou Harris & Associates for the Families and Work Institute. Funded by numerous major corporations, the five-year study sought in-depth information from nearly three thousand salaried and hourly employees. How tough are today's jobs?

Work "very hard"	88%
Work "very fast"	68%
Still don't get work done	60%
Difficulty coping	13%
Feel "used up"	71%

The research concluded that "workers are more frazzled, insecure, and torn between work and family than they were in 1977."[4] "There's a tremendous stress level, and something has to give," according to Linda Hall of Ceridian Performance Partners, which works with corporations on human resources issues.[5]

The reasons for more work and less free time are many, including the effort of many companies to raise profitability by simultaneously decreasing payroll and increasing productivity.

For a whole array of economic and sociological reasons, women have entered the workforce in large numbers so that both husbands and wives are employed outside the home. While work hours have increased, home responsibilities have stayed the same or increased. Many children are in daycare, but parents may be forced to take off work when a child becomes ill. Interestingly, 37 percent of workers said they took time off to care for their parents.[6] Many adults are "sandwiched" between children at home who need care and aging parents who also need care. The stereotypical traditional family with father going off to work and mother staying home with children has dropped to only 7 percent of employees.[7]

If the number of hours in the week stays the same but the number of hours at work increases, where is the difference made up? One place is with less sleep.

Sleeping Less

According to *USA Today*, "Americans trade sleep for work, television and other activities. . . . Right now, Americans average seven hours of sleep a night, a third get six hours or less. . . . Most people need eight hours a night to be at their best the next day and not experience a significant midafternoon drop in alertness and energy."[8]

The following sample of sleep statistics hints at the extent and seriousness of the shortage of Americans' sleep.[9]

Americans in nontraditional work schedules that interfere with natural sleep routines	25 million
Serious sleep disorders	40 million
Chronic insomnia	20 million
Sleep apnea	10–12 million
Average hours of sleep needed (adults)	8 hours per night
Average hours of actual sleep (adults)	6.7 hours per night
Cost of sleep problems to industry	$100 billion per year
Police-reported motor vehicle crashes related to driver sleepiness	100,000 per year

For those who haven't dozed off, what is the explanation for so much sleepiness? "In the big picture, sleep has a low priority (for many people)," according to Thomas Roth of the Henry Ford Hospital in Detroit. "When something has to give, sleep gives."[10]

Less sleep strains relationships, downgrades accuracy and efficiency, and otherwise lowers quality of life. Apparently it is a foolish exchange to make. According to sleep specialist and author James Maas, "People would actually be more efficient and productive if they got enough sleep."[11]

People are working more and sleeping less. Our lives are full. And, as strange as this may sound, many of us are proud of our busyness.

Busyness as a Value

"Thank you for taking time from your busy schedule" is one of the more frequent comments I hear. Thank-you notes frequently include that sentence, and people mean it as a compliment. It is their subtle way of telling me that I am important because my schedule is so full. They "honor" my importance by acknowledging my "busyness," as I have "honored" them by allocating some time from my busy schedule for them, which said to them that I consider them to be very important.

A retiring CEO from a large Christian organization bragged that he hadn't taken a vacation in twenty-seven years. Maybe he should have been confronted for defying the biblical principle of Sabbath-taking.

To not be busy is considered almost dishonorable. Would you want treatment by a surgeon who has this afternoon free and will be glad to operate on you whenever you want? Of course not. We all want a surgeon who is booked solid. Many of us would rather wait in pain for a month and be operated on by a busy physician than have relief this week through surgery by a not-so-busy doctor. Busyness is evidence of competence and a sign of success.

Who commends sleep? Who values rest? Busyness is what is important, maybe even more important than productivity or effectiveness or godliness. Busyness has become a virtue.

Impact on Churches

Churches are volunteer organizations that depend on the schedule and loyalty of parishioners. If people don't want to participate, there is no church. If they don't have the time to participate, the church changes to fit their schedules.

The impact is being seen in a list of church changes:

- *Sunday evening church services* have rapidly declined in attendance and existence among those denominations that have maintained a tradition of Sunday evening services. Sunday night is when families get together and close out everyone else. It is the time to get ready for the next school day or the new workweek.

- *Short-term commitments have replaced long-term commitments.* Many churches no longer recruit Sunday school teachers for a year at a time but for a quarter at a time or even a month at a time. Some teachers agree to show up on alternate weekends for their classes. Vacation Bible schools are five days in duration whereas once they were two weeks. Vocalists are more likely to sing for a special concert than to sing every Sunday in a choir. Board members increasingly choose shorter rather than longer terms of office.

- *Preparation time is shrinking.* Some Sunday school curriculum publishers who survey their customers admit that the preparation time for teachers is fifteen minutes or less. Many teachers do not prepare at all. Some prepare during the sermon preceding the class they teach. One of the selection criteria for Sunday school curricula and other resources is ease and shortness of preparation time.

- *Church activities are selectively attended.* A friend told me that his father attended every public meeting his church held over a fifty-year period! He didn't miss one church service, prayer meeting, business meeting, potluck dinner, Sunday school picnic, wedding, or funeral. He was unusual even in the twentieth century, but his kind is unlikely to exist in the twenty-first. Personal schedules are so crowded that everything must be prioritized, and Sunday school picnics are likely to lose out to mowing the lawn or going for a

family bike ride. More and more church activities are
viewed as optional.

- *Sunday has become a day of catch-up.* Parents come home
  tired Monday through Friday. If they can handle all the ur-
  gencies and emergencies, spend a little time with family
  members, and "unwind" in front of the television set before
  going to bed, they consider it a good evening. Personal,
  family, and household chores are postponed until the weekend. That leaves Saturday and Sunday for catching up on
  lawn mowing, grocery shopping, bill paying, home repairs,
  exercise, and sleep. Because loss of sleep is cumulative,[12]
  people need weekends to catch up so they can enter the next
  week rested.

- *Churches have to compete.* Churches have always had competition, but it has changed. When time is at a premium and
  the same or greater value can be attained from a neighborhood Bible study, personal spiritual time, a religious television program, or a nonchurch interdenominational retreat, people will go where they perceive they are getting the
  greatest value and convenience for the least expenditure of
  time.

Leading Busy Followers

Leaders of busy followers have some lessons to learn. They
are lessons of understanding, teaching, motivation, and example.

Busy people are not necessarily less committed

Do not assume a direct correlation between busyness and
level of commitment. Just because a couple is too busy to attend
an evening church service, teach a Sunday school class, or serve
on a church committee does not mean they are defective Christians or that their generation lacks the commitment of earlier
generations. Make a comparison:

Yesterday's Priorities	Today's Priorities
Institutional	Individual
Church	Family
Duty	Opportunity
Showing-up	Significance
Faithfulness	Effectiveness

This is not saying that adults in the 1950s didn't care about their families or effectiveness any more than it is saying that adults today don't value the church or faithfulness. The difference is in priorities. Today's parents may decide that it is more important to spend Sunday evening at home with their children and get them to bed early on a night before school than it is to return to the church building a second time on Sunday. The mother of grade school children may decide to take five years off from teaching Sunday school so that she can take a job in order for her children to get a better education in a private Christian school. The father in the same family may conclude that Tuesday nights are better spent with his aging parents than sitting in a church committee meeting. Frankly, it is difficult to fault Christians who give priority to their children and parents.

On the other hand, sometimes a lack of participation is evidence of a lack of commitment. Actor and director Woody Allen says that "80 percent of success is showing up." The Christian who alleges commitment but never shows up probably has a serious problem and needs help. The leader must make a judgment about followers and the connection between their priorities and their commitment.

Leadership is by example

Many followers learn more from the example of their leader than from any other source. If the leader has misdirected priorities, so will the followers. If the leader values busyness, so will the followers. Blessed is the Christian leader who understands and models *stewardship*—that is, who lives with the conviction that we are managers of God's assets, which include time. Our 168 hours each week belong to God. We cannot increase or decrease the number of hours. Our challenge is to use them in the way God wants them to be used. Although there are many aspects to this stewardship, the Sabbath principle is certainly one of the most important.

Exodus 20:8–11 is the most familiar statement of the Sabbath principle because it is part of the Ten Commandments:

> Remember the Sabbath day by keeping it holy. Six days you shall labor and do all your work, but the seventh day is a Sabbath to the Lord your God. On it you shall not do any work, neither you, nor your son or daughter, nor your manservant or maidservant, nor your animals, nor the alien within your gates. For in six days the Lord made the heavens and the earth, the sea, and all that is in them, but he rested on the seventh day. Therefore the Lord blessed the Sabbath day and made it holy.

Although it is true that this is the only commandment not specifically restated and endorsed by Jesus, it is equally true that the principle is biblical and greater than the Ten Commandments. God himself rested and set apart the seventh day in the creation narrative of Genesis 2:2–3.[13]

The Sabbath principle is expressed in Jubilee Years when the land was to lie fallow. So be like God, take a rest, give your employees a rest, give your animals a rest, and give the land a rest.

As a pastor, I can't get much rest on Sunday. And those of us who have Saturday evening worship services can't rest on Saturday either. So I rest on other days. Without being legalistic about the day or time, it's important to take a break, to take a rest, to not be "busy" at least for a day. "But how will all the work get done?" The question is not new. Hebrew farmers three thousand years ago must have asked it often: "If I don't plow, plant, or harvest in the seventh year, how am I going to eat and provide for my family?" The spiritual answer was "Trust God!" It takes great trust to believe that you can make in six-sevenths of the time what takes everyone else seven-sevenths. Let's admit it, constant busyness is personal and public evidence that we do not trust God to provide. Priorities, schedules, and Sabbaths are outward demonstrations of trust in the Lord.

Most people have to see it to believe it. The leader is the one to show them how it is done.

More must be done with less

If the needs have increased and the available time has decreased, the choices are few: (1) work more; (2) do less; (3) do more with less.

Churches are frequent examples of the 20/80 phenomenon. Twenty percent of the people do 80 percent of the work. What happens if the 20 percent do less? Either it won't get done or volunteers from the 80 percent will do it. There will never be a day when the work is spread equitably over 100 percent of the people, but leaders know that many people neither volunteer nor participate because they are crowded out of ministry by the faithful few who have always done it all and who want to do it all (even while grumbling about having to do it all).

Doing more with less requires prioritization. What won't be done? Nonprofit organizations are weak at asking the tough question, "What can we do without?" They tend to proliferate programs and continue them long after they have lost their usefulness. A preliminary first step is to decide what can go and be willing to pay the price of misunderstanding by those who want to hang on no matter how ineffective a program has become. Consider the challenging task of "zero-based programming"— listing every program now running and deciding which ones are essential and which ones are not. What must the church have to get the job done? Then focus resources on the top priorities.

A creative example of doing more with less while taking advantage of American volunteerism is the crusade against highway litter. For decades, government leaders approached the problem negatively: fine those who litter (it started with roadside signs threatening twenty-five dollar fines; when that didn't work some states went as high as thousand dollar fines, which didn't work either). Then a creative Texan suggested the idea of recruiting volunteers to pick up highway litter for two-mile stretches twice a year in exchange for a roadside sign with their names on it. The success of this idea has spread across the continent. The results have been grand: (1) hundreds of millions of dollars in highway department wages have been saved; (2) roadsides are cleaner; (3) volunteers are less likely to litter and more likely to encourage others not to litter; (4) volunteers gain a sense of ownership, satisfaction, and accomplishment. More has been done with less money and fewer employees.

In the nonprofit sector the same type of success with even greater significance has come through Millard Fuller's Habitat for Humanity. Tens of thousands of houses have been refurbished or built by volunteers so that people who otherwise could not afford a home can have one of their own. Volunteers take days and weeks of vacation time to help out. Companies allow employees to take time off. Churches and businesses donate money and materials. More is being done with less money, less government involvement, and less waiting time for the new homeowners.

Churches are abandoning committees for ministry teams. The primary difference is that committees usually supervise while ministry teams do the ministry. It is church ministry by empowerment rather than by supervision. Instead of having a Christian education committee, the Sunday school teachers run the Sunday school and the youth sponsors run the youth ministry. There is no nursery committee; there is only a nursery ministry team. Maybe this is why Paul said elders should be able to teach; it keeps them from becoming just bureaucrats.

During a denominational conference near St. Louis, I led a question-and-answer session after speaking. One woman asked, "How do you suggest we get enough volunteers to fill all 67 committee positions we have in our church?" I asked her the size of her church. She answered, "Forty-four members." It is no wonder they can't fill all the committees. Does it really take 67 committee members to supervise the ministry of 44 church members? I suggested that the church abandon all committees, empower ministry teams, and change the culture of the church from talking about ministry to doing ministry. It would take some time and work to accomplish this (probably even a "committee to do away with committees"), but the result would be less time for busy people, greater fulfillment in church involvement, and more effective ministry for Christ and the church.

Focus on the needs of the person

Good leaders have a sense of the whole that those within the organization do not have. Most of us see and care only about our "part." If I work in the nursery and we're having to turn away babies due to a shortage of workers, I'm not going to be concerned that the orchestra is short of string players. If I work in college fund-raising, I'm not too concerned about the working conditions of the dishwashers in the food service department. If I teach sociology, I'm not all that interested in the cost of microscopes for the biology labs. But the pastor of the church and the president of the college have to be concerned about the whole organization. One of the great distinctions of top leaders is their sense of the whole and their responsibility for the whole. No one sees it or experiences it in quite the same way.

In busy times, however, the leader must not forget the needs of the individual. This is not to say that one individual is more important than everyone else. In fact, there may be times when the needs and interests of certain individuals must be sacrificed for the greater good. However, leaders who focus on the needs of an individual may be able to meet the person's needs and the organization's needs at the same time. When dealing with busy people who have demands coming at them from every direction, effective leaders will ask themselves, *Who is this person? What does she need most? How can I help her meet her needs through our church?*

Followers must be rewarded

We usually think of donors writing the checks to us, not our writing checks to them. Churches don't have the resources to pay every Sunday school teacher, usher, musician, or board member. Besides, we're talking about organizations that are legally not-for-profit. We can't pay.

Busy people value every hour. They have only a few discretionary hours available to give each week. They will give those hours where they get "paid" the most. If that's in a church service, that's where they will go. If it's staying home watching television, that's where they will stay.

The currency is not cash; it's challenge, growth, peace, comfort, information, encounter with God, friendships, signifi-

cance, satisfaction, and all of the other important things money
can't buy.

The twenty-first century leader will pay followers very well.
Otherwise they will quit. There just isn't time to waste. There
are too many other options to choose from.

Chapter 6

Options—Living in a Catalog Culture

HENRY FORD offered the Model T in any color the customer wanted, as long as it was black. If Henry Ford tried doing business that way today, Henry Ford would be out of business.

North American society has become a culture of choices. We have so many alternatives that we take them for granted. If anything, we are surprised when the options are limited.

- *Service stations.* Gasoline is sold in at least three grades: unleaded, unleaded plus, and premium; larger stations offer at least one type of diesel fuel; and many offer LP (liquid petroleum) and kerosene. Every station is expected to have public rest rooms. Most sell candy, magazines, groceries, fast food, auto supplies, and long-distance phone cards. Some have a sit-down restaurant. Payment may be made by cash, check, or credit card (Visa, Master-Card, Discover, American Express, Diner's Club, government card, oil company card, or others). And a significant number of the stations are open 24 hours a day, 365 days a year, for your convenience.
- *Supermarkets.* The typical supermarket carries at least fifty

thousand items for sale. In addition to availability, each item comes in numerous varieties. Hot dogs are available frozen or refrigerated; in packs of four, eight, twelve or more; made out of pork, beef, turkey, or a combination; they can be smoked or nonsmoked, kosher or nonkosher, high fat or low fat or no fat, short or long, fat or thin. Mustard comes in big bottles and little bottles; in glass containers, plastic containers, or squeeze tubes; yellow or brown; mild or medium or hot; imported or domestic. Cereal is available from General Mills, Post, Kellogg, Quaker, and other manufacturers, as well as generic house brands. It is made from wheat, rice, oats, and other products; it is sugar-coated or sugar-free; it's sold in institutional size, family size, regular size, or individual serving size; it comes with raisins, blueberries, other additions, or plain; it can be bought ready to eat or ready to prepare; some is to be served hot, some is to be served cold; some is packaged for children, some for adults. Toilet paper (which newcomers to the United States have told me has the most amazing and disconcerting array of alternatives they have ever seen) comes in single-ply, double-ply, or multiple-ply; patterned, colored, or plain; generic or name brand; smooth or embossed; single- or double-size rolls; packages of one, two, four, eight, twelve, sixteen, or more rolls; septic-tank safe or use only with city sewer systems.

- *Long-distance telephone service.* The big names in long-distance phone service are AT&T, MCI, and Sprint, but many smaller companies offer competitive and comparable service. When you select your long-distance carrier, you must also choose which plan you prefer. Do you want a single-rate service twenty-four hours a day or service that charges higher rates during business hours and lower rates at night and on weekends; a calling card feature that allows you to charge calls from other telephones; single or multiple lines; a toll-free number so your children or others may call you at no charge to them; call-waiting, caller ID, voice mail, customized ringing, call forwarding, home phone repair service, or mobile-phone-same-number service, all of which are available through your local or regional telephone company but not from the long-distance company (well, at least not in most places)?

Consider the fictional but typical story of Herbert, who signed up for AT&T long-distance service. He was quite satisfied until he received a letter from Sprint offering him $50 to switch carriers (and also promising to pay the switch charge and handle all the arrangements), so he switched to Sprint. Several weeks later he received a check in the mail from MCI. All he needed to do was sign and cash the check and he would be switched from Sprint to MCI. Grateful for the cash, Herbert endorsed the check and went straight to his bank for a deposit. Early the next month he received a call from AT&T saying how much they missed him and offering him $100 if he would switch back. Immediately deciding that he missed AT&T as much as they missed him, Herbert agreed and was right back where he started—but $225 richer. The funny part of the story is that Herbert doesn't know anyone outside of his area code and hasn't made a long-distance phone call in the past two years.

Compared to people living a generation ago, we have a breathtaking array of choices in magazines, television stations (including cable and satellite dish services), automobile brands, restaurants, barbershops, mutual funds, insurance policies, clothes, careers, discount stores, airfares, computers, styles of music and the means to hear it (concerts, radio, television, cassette tapes, and compact discs), and over-the-counter pain relievers.

When options are limited, there is a public outcry. We see this happening in the health-care industry because health maintenance organizations (HMOs) have limited the choice of physicians and specialists available to their members.

Choice Has Penetrated the Culture

Choice has become as much a part of the American culture as paved roads, indoor plumbing, and reading and writing. Although some citizens still live and travel on dirt roads, have outhouses, and can't read or write, they are the exceptions. The same is true of choice. It's so common we don't think about it. We take it for granted. Choice is normal, the way things are supposed to be. In fact, it's the lack of choice that seems strange.

Imagine going into a shoe store at a suburban shopping

mall. A very gracious young salesperson greets you and offers to help. You explain that your running shoes are wearing out and you want to buy a new pair. He offers you a seat and walks to the back room, picks up a box of shoes, and brings them out for you to see. They are size 10 C, high-cut basketball shoes on sale for $99. "They look good," you say, "but I wear a size 12 D, and I prefer low-cut. Besides, I want running shoes, not basketball shoes, and I don't want to spend more than $75, including tax." Smiling, the salesperson responds, "These are really good shoes, and our research shows that they are the most popular size and style. The price is very good too."

What would you do? No doubt, you'd get up and walk out without making a purchase. As you leave you may think, "He was a nice guy and the store is nice, but they don't care about me. It doesn't make any difference to them what I need or want. All they care about is what they want to sell."

The same thing happens in churches. Visitors discover that the ministry is designed for someone else. If they don't speak our language, wear our style of clothes, like our style of music, or know our prayers and creeds, and if they can't locate a Bible reference by book and chapter or come at a time convenient to us, the message is clear: "Change to be like us, because we're never going to change to meet your needs." Is it any wonder that visitors think, *"They don't care about me; it doesn't make any difference to them what I need or want; all they care about is the way they already do things"*?

Where there is no choice offered, it appears as if no one really cares.

Churches and Choices

Wooddale Church, where I am the pastor, offers five weekend worship services. The first is a contemporary style service on Saturday evening at 5:15. On Sunday morning there are four services scheduled: 8:30, 9:30, 9:50, and 11:15. Two are contemporary and two are traditional. Three are held in the Worship Center and one is held in the Great Room. The traditional services feature a robed choir, orchestra, hymns, and a world-class pipe organ. The contemporary services feature a worship team of instrumentalists and singers and lots of congregational singing with words projected on screens. In general, worshipers dress up for the traditional services and dress more casually for the contemporary services. The theme and sermon are the same in all services.

I've had people tell me that such a variety of choices in times, locations, and styles is an example of the worst of religious accommodation to selfish American consumerism. "People should learn to bend their schedules and preferences to the church and not the other way around," they argue.

Let's consider that idea in light of what we know about the New Testament Gospels. Those who have read the New Testament straight through know that Matthew includes many references and allusions to the Old Testament (which is fine if you're familiar with the Old Testament but difficult if you're not). Next you read Mark and think, "This is very familiar; it's almost as if I read it all quite recently." That's because 95 percent of the content of Mark is in Matthew. Then you read Luke, and it's not a whole lot different from Matthew and Mark. But John is very different with its new teachings, new stories, and fresh approach. Bible scholars call Matthew, Mark, and Luke the Synoptic Gospels because they are so much alike (like words that are synonyms). John, the only non-synoptic gospel, was written later and includes material that doesn't appear in the first three gospels.

Why isn't there just one gospel of our Lord Jesus Christ? Why do we need four biographies of Jesus, when any one of them tells all the essential information? Why couldn't God get the story right in one attempt? The answer is that each gospel targets a different audience. Matthew is written to a Hebrew audience, which knew the Old Testament and the Jewish traditions. Mark is written to a Gentile audience, which knew little or nothing about the Old Testament and Jewish traditions. The basic content of Mark is the same as Matthew, but it is shorter and skips most of the Jewish connections. Luke takes a different approach—somewhere between the first two. Luke was a physician and a scholar. His opening lines are written in a more classical style of Greek than the rest of the New Testament, and he is more thematic than chronological in telling the story of Jesus. John takes yet another approach, reporting what the others did not include and writing with a more direct evangelistic style. In fact, John says that his gospel is "written that you may believe that Jesus is the Christ, the Son of God, and that by believing you may have life in his name" (20:31).

Apparently God and the New Testament authors realized the importance of offering different options for different audiences. It's similar to offering different styles of church services at different times for different audiences.

Obviously no church can offer everything would-be parishioners need or want, any more than a single shoe store can carry every style and size needed and preferred by everyone who may at one time shop there. It is important, however, that leaders recognize the variety of needs to be met in order to reach the people they are called by God to reach. It is especially important in a culture where people are used to choice.

The Velcro Effect

Velcro holds things together by using hundreds of small hooks and eyes that catch and stick to each other. The more hooks and eyes there are, the stronger the bond when they touch.

In a church, multiple options work like Velcro. The more choices there are, the stronger the bond is likely to be between the church and the people and the longer the bond will last. Take the Modecker family as an example. Jim and Susanna have just moved to town because of a job transfer. They have three children living at home: Jeremy, seventeen, is a high school junior; Jason, fourteen, is in junior high school; and Joelene, eight, is in elementary school. Also staying with them is Susanna's twenty-six-year-old niece, Kimberley, who is just starting her career as a stockbroker. The list of what they are looking for in a church is too long to print here. It is actually six lists with some areas of overlap. They have expectations about music, Bible teaching, theology, friendships, Sunday school, youth ministry, service opportunities, and small groups. They do not expect a church to have everything they want any more than they expected to find a house that satisfied everyone's needs, wants, and expectations. But the more they can get the better. If Joelene likes her Sunday school teacher and makes friends, if Jason fits into the junior high youth groups and sees students who attend his school, if Jeremy likes the senior high youth group and starts dating a girl from the church, if Kimberley joins the contemporary music team and finds a short-term foreign missions project she can participate in as part of the singles group, if Susanna joins a weekly women's Bible study and makes new friends with similar spiritual interests, and if Jim is spiritually and intellectually challenged by the pastor's Sunday morning sermons, they will stick to this church. But what will happen if Joelene's favorite Sunday school teacher quits teaching and moves a thousand miles away the same week that Jeremy breaks up with his girlfriend and says he never wants to go to the senior high youth group again? The family will probably still stick, because there are so many other "hooks and eyes" connecting them to the church. Fewer choices mean fewer connections; more choices mean more connections.

Choices and Church Size

Can smaller churches offer multiple choices, or is this an option limited to megachurches with huge resources?

It is true that larger churches usually offer more options than smaller churches (which is one of the reasons they are larger and also a significant factor in their continued growth). But there are very few megachurches. If "mega" means 2000 or more in average weekly attendance, there are only about 400[1] in the entire United States out of more than 400,000 churches. Only one-tenth of 1 percent of American churches are megachurches.

At the opposite end of the size continuum was Westminster Presbyterian Church in Duluth, Minnesota. It averaged 40 at Sunday morning worship services and was on a long-term plateau in 1995 when the congregation added a second Sunday morning service. The addition was not because of lack of space; it was added to provide another option, both for present members of the church and for those they hoped to reach. During the twenty-four months following the start of the second service the congregation increased to an average Sunday morning total worship attendance of over 200.[2]

Almost any size church can stretch to add one or more options. Many larger churches have become larger because they have repeatedly stretched, adding programs just beyond their comfort zone time after time. After a while the law of compounding returns begins to take over—the larger the church, the greater the options, which grows the church so that even more options can be offered.

The adding of options does not stand as an isolated principle. This too is complex. The options added must be relevant and effective. And they need to be done with excellence.[3] Among the many regions and subcultures of North America, I have found settings where contemporary and traditional churches have flourished with the addition of liturgical services even though the church belongs to a nonliturgical denomination. High church liturgy is increasingly attractive to adults born after 1965, just as contemporary worship became popular among baby boomers born between 1946 and 1964. A ministry to single mothers is more likely to succeed in Palmdale, California, with a high percentage of single mother families than in Sun City, Arizona, where most single mothers have gained that status through widowhood, not unwed pregnancy or divorce. Just because an option is good in one place doesn't mean it is good in another. McDonald's keeps "McRib" barbecued pork sandwiches on their regular menu throughout the southeastern states because they sell well, but they only offer McRibs as an occasional special promotion in the northern states. All of which is to say that more options for their own sake is not a good idea, but more options to meet more needs can be a very good idea.

One estimate calculates that 20 percent of Americans are unable to regularly attend Sunday morning church services. The percentage is high because the reasons are many: shut-ins, parents with disabled children, caregivers to the elderly, shift workers, family members of shift workers who don't have transportation available on Sundays (most metropolitan bus systems cancel or significantly reduce their schedules on Sundays), and a whole array of people who are so tired that they sleep late on Sunday morning. If there are no evening worship services available on Saturday, Sunday (growing in popularity), or weeknights, these people will rarely or never come. Just as church buildings have increasingly become handicapped accessible, many more should become schedule accessible.

What option can a small church offer that isn't already available at the larger church across town? Ask any pastor of a large church what people say about the size of the congregation, and he will say, "It's too big!"[4] Most people are forced to choose between the small size they prefer and the greater number of services they want. When smaller churches offer more services, they have an immediate and powerful competitive edge over larger congregations. But the next problem they face is that such churches often grow larger and disappoint those who liked the church when it was smaller.

Consider two extremes. Small groups and single adults ministries are choices many seek. Singles ministries often require a critical mass of population that is greater than the average-sized church. Unless located near a university, most smaller churches are poorly positioned to have credible singles groups. The best option is to not have one. Send singles to the group in a larger church.[5] On the other hand, a church of any size can provide a small group option. The group(s) can meet weekly or monthly, in the church building or in a home, with a formal curriculum or without, with couples or individuals, by gender or mixed, generational or intergenerational.

Here is an example unrelated to church size. Early Christmas Eve services have been pioneered and popularized by churches in Georgia, Texas, and Minnesota. These churches had already established traditional candlelight services every December 24.[6] But what about all the people who travel to visit relatives over the Christmas holidays? Many of these travelers have never been to a Christmas Eve service in their home community or church. So early Christmas Eve services are now being offered on the weekend (or several days) before Christmas—perhaps on a Sunday evening. The services are exactly the same as the ones on December 24, but a few days earlier so holiday travelers can participate. This works especially well in communities with younger adults and younger families who are likely to travel during the holidays to visit parents; it doesn't work as well in communities with older adults and families who are more likely to have the out-of-town visitors come to them.

Leading in an Era of Options

Leadership is different in settings with multiple options. There is far less place for the know-it-all, do-it-all, up-front leader. The reason is obvious: no one is capable of offering all choices and participating in every option. The twenty-first century leader must see and communicate the vision of options and then enable others to create and lead those options.

Consider one leadership approach to expanding ministry options:

1. Inventory resources

When a family seeks financial counseling, the usual place to begin is by listing all assets. It's also a good place for a church to begin. Gather together a group of church members and leaders who know the church well and ask them to participate in a one-month project. The goal is to list everything the church has and does.

The list may include some or all of the following:

land	community reputation	Christmas program
building	ushers	fax
Sunday school	softball team	photocopier
Sunday services	mortgage	hymnals
pastor	denominational	Bibles
members	affiliation	curriculum
youth group	library	adult class(es)
choir	secretary	church signs
organist	parking	free newspaper ads
nursery	monthly business	insurance
missionaries	meetings	former members
$50,000 in savings	confirmation	church directory
bulletin	baptisms	special concerts
monthly newsletter	weddings	offerings
deacons	social concerns	potluck dinners
50 years of history	ministry	work days
telephone prayer	funerals	benevolence fund
chains	Communion	
VBS	bulletin boards	

In churches with greater resources, the list may include singles ministry, divorce recovery workshop, pastoral counseling, premarital counseling, missions program, senior adult ministry, special education class, marriage enrichment weekends, endowment, radio program, church bus, church van, youth pastor, Christian education director, church nurse, parochial school, cemetery, and more.

The inventory will impress almost every church that:

- the church has resources
- the church has many ministries
- resources are not equal
- resources are not focused

2. Prioritize the resources

Answer the following questions (based on the inventory list):

What does the church do best? (top 3)

1. _____

2. _____

3. _____

What does the church not do well? (bottom 3)

1. _____

2. _____

3. _____

What is absolutely necessary for our church to do? (top 3)

1. _____

2. _____

3. _____

What would we discontinue if something had to be

dropped in order for the church to survive? (choose 5)

1. _____

2. _____

3. _____

4. _____

5. _____

What should we be doing that we are not now doing? (choose 3)

1. _____

2. _____

3. _____

3. Make a plan

Recognizing that there will be resistance to discontinuing anything because almost every church activity has a vocal constituency of at least one person, start the hard work of turning priorities into a plan. Suggest that the added options be initiated on a pilot-project basis. For example, include a Christmas Eve service or an additional Christmas Eve service; add one more Sunday morning worship service at another hour for six weeks up to and including Easter; schedule one marriage enrichment weekend; start a church softball team with a goal of 50 percent unchurched players; call every newcomer to the community with a word of welcome and an invitation to a church service; plan one Mom's Day Out program; offer a free night of baby-sitting during the Christmas shopping season.

The best way to expand options is to include at least three. This increases the likelihood of success. Most people like success and dislike failure. Beware of adding a single option doomed to failure, because that may doom future attempts.

Recruit outside the central corps of faithful church workers. Be willing to recruit outside of the church. For example, ask church teenagers to sponsor the Christmastime free baby-sitting service and have them invite their unchurched friends to help out. Offer free pizza. Put a church nurse or schoolteacher in charge.

4. Decide how to finance the new options

Whenever a church or other ministry offers new options, there is a price attached. How will the price be paid?

- Stretch: contribute more time and money; involve more people.
- Replace: stop doing something less important to start doing something more important.

5. See what happens

This process has some predictable results.

- Leaders will be leading. This always changes an organization.
- There will be resistance. This is inevitable, and it's not proof of failure.
- Success tastes good. The more a church tastes, the more a church wants.
- New options will force old ministries to be neglected or to close down.
- The loss of old ministries will bring grief. Some people will grieve inappropriately.
- New options will either draw new people or increase involvement of those who are already members. Usually both.

Leaders must be wise in adding and subtracting options. It is a good time to follow the advice of James 1:5: "If any of you lacks wisdom, he should ask God, who gives generously to all without finding fault, and it will be given to him."

It is also a good time to avoid one of the most common leadership mistakes: focusing resources on weaknesses rather than on strengths. If the church is good at sports and poor at music, expand options in sports ministry. Then hope and pray that the expanded softball league will recruit some players who are also good singers (or whose spouses are). Too often organizations pour resources into what they can't do well and fail to take advantage of what they do well. In football terms, if your team is good at running the ball and poor at passing the ball, run!

The rector of a midwestern Episcopal church proposed adding another worship option to the Sunday schedule—a Sunday evening contemporary service. There was no tradition for this addition, and no one knew if anyone would come. The results were amazing. Not only was the attendance large from the first Sunday but the church gathered an array of newcomers and significantly enhanced the worship experience of those who were already members. The negative impact on the Sunday morning traditional service was none. Good idea. Good option. Good leadership. Good results.

Does it always turn out this well? Of course not. A southwestern Lutheran church added a country-western service as a new option. On paper the idea looked good. The massive popularity of country-western music in North America seemed to indicate there would be a good response. Initial enthusiasm quickly wore off. The people of the area closest to the church campus weren't country-western fans. The service was discontinued. Good idea. Good option. Good leadership. Not so good results. However, the attempt was a positive experience for the congregation and it smoothed the way for future additional options.

Chapter 7

Competition—Like Running a Marathon

MORE THAN ONE HUNDRED YEARS ago the U.S. Congress granted major league baseball an exemption from America's antimonopoly laws. Technically, this means they have no competition. While that may have been true at one time, today it is a joke.

In 1950 there were ten cities with one or more major league baseball teams. St. Louis was the farthest west. There were over 400 minor league semi-professional teams. Since then the population of the United States has nearly doubled but the number of minor league teams has dropped below 200. Baseball is still popular but hardly "the national pastime" it once was. Most stadiums seldom fill to capacity for games. Children are more and more likely to play soccer or basketball than baseball.

Blame the change on players' strikes. Blame it on the preference for more "active" sports. Blame it on free agency, which moves players from team to team, reducing fan loyalty. Blame it on the inability of smaller cities to field financially viable franchises compared to larger cities like New York and Los Angeles.

Most of all, blame it on competition. Not baseball compe-

tition, but other competition. Since 1950 the success and popularity of the NBA, NFL, and NHL have brought millions of
fans into major league sports. Soccer is booming in popularity
among younger Americans, predicting a healthy future for the
world's most popular competitive sport.

In other words, major league baseball was granted a monopoly that worked against it rather than for it in an increasingly
competitive culture. The same goes for the church.

Many denominations have strict franchise systems. If there
is already a Roman Catholic, Episcopal, Methodist, Presbyterian, or Lutheran church in a community of a certain size, there
won't be another one to compete with it. The first church in
town has a monopoly. Guaranteed success? Hardly. As soon as
the town starts to grow, new churches start. They may be
Assemblies of God, Baptist, Wesleyan, or a different brand of
Lutheran or Presbyterian. The most likely to start fresh is a
nondenominational church. In a highly competitive environment, the established church may flounder while the fledgling
church flourishes.

Competition doesn't come only from other churches. It
comes from television, sports, school, employment, family
functions, fatigue, home maintenance, hobbies, and apathy.
This has made church leadership more interesting and more
difficult. Long gone are the days when church leaders could
function in a noncompetitive, business-as-usual monopoly.
Those who still do often lose their constituency, fail their mission, and close the church. According to Lyle Schaller,

> Today the level of competition among congregations to
> reach and attract the younger generation of churchgoers is
> at a level unprecedented in American history. This fact of
> life is decried by almost everyone except the active church
> shoppers, some of whom are newcomers to the community,
> while others are long time residents who have decided the
> time has come to search for a new church home.[1]

America's Fastest Growing Denomination

An interesting comparison can be made between the United
Methodist Church, with 33,265 churches, and the Southern

Baptist Convention, with 38,867 churches.[2] The Southern Baptist Convention became America's largest Protestant denomination in 1963 when it reached 10.4 million members and surpassed the United Methodist Church.[3] Historically, Methodists were the most aggressive church planters. There are more towns with Methodist churches than there are towns with United States Post Offices. However, the Methodists neglected to continue church planting and the Southern Baptists aggressively pursued it.

This bodes well for the Southern Baptists but is ominous for the United Methodists because the future probably belongs to those starting the most new churches. Like people, churches have life cycles. This means that most of the churches still existing in the year 2025 will be those that started between 1975 and 2024. Since the Southern Baptists started the most churches in the twentieth century, they will have a large and growing market share in the twenty-first. Most mainline denominations are starting comparatively few new churches. Some close more than they open.

The fastest growing denomination in the United States isn't a denomination at all, at least not technically. The fastest growing "denomination" is nondenominational churches and churches that function as if they were nondenominational. There are more people at worship services each weekend in these churches than in any denomination in the country.[4] And the number is growing rapidly.

These churches fit a broad array of descriptions:

- churches that have split off from denominational churches over doctrine, life-style, personality, or other issues and have chosen not to affiliate with another denomination[5]
- churches being started by entrepreneurial, independent church planters who are more focused on mission than affiliation
- ethnic churches that are identified by race, language, and country of origin more than by denominational doctrines or affiliations
- megachurches that sense no value in denominational affiliation or consider denominations to be a hindrance to their missions

- independent churches that use quasi-denominational labels. There are many churches that call themselves "Baptist" or "Christian" or "Pentecostal" but have no tie to organized denominations using the same names. There are more than 21,000 "other" Baptist churches, 6,800 "other" Pentecostal churches, and 15,000 "other" Christian churches listed among national denominational statistics
- storefront churches that are unaware of the possibility of denominational connection
- nonreporting denominational churches that have never severed their official denominational connection but operate completely independently
- "daughter churches" of independent or independent-like churches that have never considered the possibility of a denominational affiliation

The number becomes even larger when the list is expanded to include church associations that have grown out of local megachurches like Calvary Chapel and The Vineyard.

Not all independent churches thrive or even survive. Three out of five new churches started in the United States fail within five years. That's a 60 percent mortality rate. But new businesses in the United States have an 80 percent five-year mortality rate, so new churches have a better survival rate than businesses.

Churches that do survive thrive at an astonishing rate. They are young, flexible, aggressive, populist, and mobile. Unlike many denominational churches that simply transplanted their European heritage, these are highly indigenous, "made in the USA" churches. They are unencumbered by ecclesiastical structures, don't have to pay denominational assessments, aren't forced to conform to historic clergy credentialing, and usually have little concern for the way things have always been done. On the other side, these churches risk instability, isolation, heterodoxy, and a host of other potential ills. However they are described, they are a phenomenon making a significant contribution to the competition among North American churches.

Denominationalism

Some denominations remain strong. Surveys of church leaders and analyses of church attendance patterns overwhelmingly affirm the strength of denominational churches in North America. This can be very confusing when we hear that denominationalism is on a steep decline. Which is it? Strength or decline? The answer is "both."

I met this confusion head on after one Sunday morning worship service. A man waiting to speak to me said he had something to tell me. His words were carefully chosen. He said, "I just want you to know three things about me. I love Jesus Christ. I love Wooddale Church. I will always be a Roman Catholic." That's an interesting statement to make to a Protestant pastor, but not off-base. His first loyalty is to Jesus Christ and not to any church or denomination. He found a fulfilling and growing spiritual experience at Wooddale Church and loves what he experiences. He was born and raised a Roman Catholic and will always consider himself a Roman Catholic even if he never participates in any way.

Denominational loyalty is both a help and a hindrance to many churches. It is helpful in keeping members, because many people would never consider going to a church of another denomination. Those who were born and raised Lutheran or Catholic may be "good Catholics" or "good Lutherans" who attend services and try to keep the rules or they may be absentee Catholics or Lutherans who show up once a year or never. But they are still Catholics or Lutherans. To change churches would be as unthinkable as changing citizenship or gender or race. They were born into the church and that's what they are. This virtually guarantees the indefinite survival of many large historic denominations. It explains the enormous numerical growth of attendance at many large urban Catholic churches that are booming because of the return of young adults who were born and raised Catholics. When they finally get around to returning to religion, they only think of one choice.

The hindrance comes from modern eclecticism and ecumenism. Millions of North Americans are religiously eclectic in that they choose their beliefs a la carte rather than from a cohesive system. They see nothing inconsistent about going to a Pentecostal church and still calling themselves Catholics. They can have loyalty and variety at the same time. They are ecumenical in the sense that grass-roots tolerance and acceptance of other denominations is at an all-time high. The doctrinal differences among denominations are considered to be man-made and relatively unimportant. Beliefs are personal. Someone can attend a church and agree with 50 percent of what the church teaches and disagree with the other 50 percent.

The result of this fluctuating denominationalism is escalated competition between churches.

Other Religions

Most North American churches were born into a culture of Christian dominance. The only question was *which* church or *which* denomination. The only serious alternative was Judaism, and few converted to it. Churches recruited from those born into their denomination or from those born into other Christian traditions. Non-Christian religions were competition only in far away countries and cultures.

According to Diana L. Eck, "The significant immigration of non-Christians has caused a growing pluralization of previously majority-Christian Canada and the United States. There are literally hundreds of temples, monasteries, mosques, and centers throughout the United States." She concludes that "the plurality of religious traditions and cultures challenges people in every part of the world today, including the United States, which is now the most religiously diverse country on earth."[6]

Christian leadership is different in a diverse and religiously pluralistic culture. Leaders must be aware of what is happening and interpret those happenings to the church. On one hand, we must demonstrate Christian attitudes and actions toward those whose beliefs and lifestyles are different from ours. On the other hand, we must be strategic in our efforts to evangelize those who are not Christians. This is not dissimilar to the role and relationships of the early Christian church in the religiously diverse Roman Empire. It is, however, very dissimilar to the way a majority of Christian church members see their churches, culture, and country. As one person put it, "I used to think that a religiously mixed marriage was uniting a Methodist with a Baptist. Now it's a Catholic with a Muslim."

Ethnic Change

Much of the new religious pluralism comes from immigration, which raises calls for new laws to keep foreigners out. People fear that outsiders will change us to be like them. In reality, the greater threat may be the other way around.

Look at what is happening from a sociological point of view. There is a tidal wave of power in cultural majority. Minorities struggle to maintain their culture, language, traditions, and religion into the second and third generation after immigration. It is more likely that the minority will become like the majority than the other way around. When the son or grandson of a Muslim immigrant gets a scholarship to a major southeastern university and starts to date a Southern Baptist coed from Georgia, the odds are greater that he will want to become a Baptist than that she will want to become a Muslim. To one degree or another, that story will be repeated millions of times. Some will retain their religious and cultural heritage. Most will not. In fact, the immigrant groups have established large and expanding Christian churches. Some were Christian before coming to North America, but many have converted since immigration.

The largest change is happening among the Spanish-speaking population. Although traditionally Roman Catholic, millions are changing to Protestant churches, especially those with Pentecostal leanings. Hispanic churches are such a large growth industry for some Protestant denominations that they account for all of the denominations' increases over the past decade. If it weren't for Hispanic churches, they would have declined.

In 1995, 26.8 million Hispanics were in the United States, and by 2010 there are expected to be 40.5 million, a 51 percent increase. The twelve states with the largest Hispanic populations are California, Texas, Florida, New York, Illinois, Arizona, New Jersey, New Mexico, Colorado, Massachusetts, Washington, and Pennsylvania. Churches in these states have been and will continue to be greatly affected, while churches in North Dakota, a very large state, will hardly notice the growth from 7,000 to 9,000 Hispanics.[7]

The Caucasian segment of the American population, on the other hand, is experiencing a zero percent population growth. Between 1990 and 2000 the Caucasian population shrank from 76 to 72 percent and is projected to fall to 62 percent by 2025.[8] Hispanics are very close to surpassing blacks as the nation's largest minority group, according to the United States Census Bureau. By 2050, people of Hispanic origin will constitute 24.5 percent of the population. In past generations, the immigrant language has disappeared and been replaced by English. That may well happen with Spanish language speakers as well. The process is being slowed, however, by the large numbers of those who speak Spanish and by the massive effort of businesses to accommodate customers who speak Spanish. Across the southern United States, the Yellow Pages are available in Spanish, there are more than four hundred Spanish language radio stations, and Univision and Telemundo are the top-rated Spanish television networks. Major sports events are now televised in English and Spanish with instructions to touch a special remote control button to choose your preferred language. There is far less motivation for Spanish speakers to learn English than there was for speakers of other languages in earlier generations.

Just as businesses are reaching out to customers in Spanish, churches must do the same.[9]

Money

The rich are getting richer. The poor are getting poorer. The middle class is shrinking. North American churches have been mostly middle class. The competition for dollars is one of the significant leadership challenges facing the twenty-first century church.

Who has the money? Half of all the wealth in the United States is owned by 3.5 percent of the population.[10] According to an analysis by the Knight Ridder News Service, "In the course of a generation, the percentage of tax-filers who are working poor has grown by one-sixth; the percentage who are in the middle class has shrunk by nearly one-fifth; and the percentage who are well-off has doubled."[11]

What about churches too poor to survive? The Atlantic provinces of Canada have been repeatedly buffeted by economic difficulties. Barry Dixon of the United Baptist Convention of the Atlantic Provinces explains the challenge:

> It's been said that money makes the world go round. It shouldn't come as a surprise that even churches need money in order to operate. An increasing number of small and/or rural churches are finding that there simply isn't enough money to maintain the work. In a sense, some churches have dropped below a sort of poverty line. The label seems harsh, but it is the unfortunate reality.
>
> At what point does a church drop below this poverty line? Generally (and there are exceptions), the poverty line for an Atlantic Baptist church, or for a combined pastorate, falls somewhere in the $45,000 to $50,000 [Canadian dollars] annual income range.[12]

These numbers represent the minimum salary, housing, and benefits required to support a full-time pastor, as well as the "bare bones" costs of maintaining the average church. Congregations whose annual incomes fall below $45,000 are most likely below the poverty line.[13]

When churches fall below the poverty line they start focusing more on survival than on mission. Pressuring members to give more seldom works because to them giving doesn't seem to make any difference. Other churches are functionally below the poverty line even though they technically have enough income. Their problem is unwise spending. Some give so much to missions, social ministries, and denominational assessments that they underpay the pastor and allow the building to deteriorate. Eventually they reach the point where it is impossible to call or keep a quality pastor and the building is in such disrepair that fixing it is impractical.

Barry Dixon goes beyond bemoaning the problem and offers some practical solutions for poor rural churches in the Atlantic provinces. He recommends that key layleaders form a "Future of Our Church Committee" to study the challenges

and consider the options. The committee should pray, get outside counsel, and consider alternatives such as licensing a member who is a schoolteacher as a bivocational lay pastor, calling
a retired pastor as a long-term interim, or sharing a pastor with
another area church. Dixon says that "when a church falls
below the poverty line, a radically different approach to ministry may need to be considered, but it need not mean the de-
mise of the church itself. Remember, no matter what the circumstances, the Lord specializes in turning difficulties into His
victories."[14]

Money problems are not limited to the poor. It is possible
to have huge resources and still go out of business. The Tandy
Corporation (best known for its Radio Shack chain of retail
electronics stores) launched seventeen huge Incredible Universe superstores with 184,000 square feet each of retail space.
That is bigger than four football fields of consumer electronics.
"Our customers liked us but we needed more of them," according to Tandy spokesman Martin Moad. "Incredible Universe has a lot of positives to it, but when you really get down
to it, it's really not making any money." The decision to close
down these superstores was financial. Even the biggest and best
are competing for money.[15]

One of the largest churches in the Midwest was the flagship
congregation of its denomination. Yet despite its rich history,
strategic location, and significant financial resources, it is on the
verge of closure due to poor planning. A committee studied the
aging of the members, the declining of the attendance, the
mounting estimates for repairs to their historic building, and
actually projected the "date of no return" a decade in advance.
The committee proposed plans for sale of the property and relocation, along with a whole strategy for effective future ministry. The congregation received the report and went on with
business as usual for the next ten years. Now the numbers are
too few, the income too low, and the property worth far less. It
may be too late.

A Southern California church received national attention as
one of the largest and fastest growing churches in America.
Then the pastor was accused of sexual immorality. He denied
the accusations but still resigned, and people started leaving.

The church called a new pastor who brought commitment and skill but also inexperience and poor health to this already difficult situation. Within a few years there wasn't enough income to pay the mortgage, sustain the facility, pay the staff, and continue the program. Merger with a nearby congregation was the only solution.

The point of these illustrations is to show that a church, even though it is many other things, is also a business. Businesses require wise financial management. Today's church leader must either give wise financial management or see to it that someone else does.

Ironically, one of the more common religious myths is that "a church is not a business and should not be run like a business." That borders on nonsense. Of course the church is not a business like AT&T or IBM. Of course the church is not a business that is owned by stockholders who expect a financial return on their investment. Of course a church does not sell a tangible product, pay sales representatives, own warehouses, or have a listing on the New York Stock Exchange. But a church is a business in that the checkbook must balance, the deed to the property must be registered, the utility bills must be paid, payroll taxes must be withheld and paid, and the money going out must not exceed the money coming in. In our culture, these are matters of law. Failure to run the business side of the church by established accounting standards could result in bankruptcy, maybe even prison.

The church is also a business in that it must compete for dollars. Virtually every donor in every church is multiply solicited to contribute to other religious and charitable causes. Some will give out of guilt; some will give out of loyalty; more and more will give out of opportunity. Individuals will decide for themselves how they will distribute their charitable dollars. One of the top reasons people give to a church or other ministry is confidence in the leadership.

Fascinating new generational forces are both helping and hindering church financial stability. For example, congregations switching from traditional music to contemporary music may lose older members to other congregations. In many churches, long-standing traditions are being funded by the proceeds of wills from dying members while more contemporary churches are financially strapped. Another spin on the situation comes from differing motivations to give. The generosity of the pre–World War II generation has been motivated by loyalty and survival. The generosity of the post–World War II generation is more likely to be motivated by opportunity and success. The church leader who writes a monthly fund-raising letter that appeals to loyalty and warns of disaster may attract gifts from those born before 1940 but actually alienate those born after 1950. Younger donors interpret institutional crises differently, wondering why they should contribute to a sinking ship. They prefer to give their money to causes that seize exciting opportunities and to organizations that have a track record of success. The leader needs to know the audience and relate generationally to be effective.

Church Size

Just as there is a shrinking socioeconomic middle class in North America, there is also a shrinking midsize church in America. It is increasingly difficult for a congregation to maintain an average weekend worship attendance of 100–150. Midsize churches are increasingly becoming either smaller or larger.

Church growth expert Lyle Schaller has analyzed the Evangelical Lutheran Church in America (ELCA) and other denominations. He says that churchgoers are concentrated in a comparatively small number of larger churches. "The combined average worship attendance of the nine largest parishes was approximately 25,000 in 1994, the same as the combined average worship attendance for the smallest 979 congregations."[16]

Large churches provide the quality and quantity of services many people are seeking. Examples include programs for disabled teenagers, substance-abuse recovery groups, blended-family Sunday school classes, graduate-school-level theology courses, licensed counseling, prayer groups for mothers of teenagers, and more. Larger churches not only have the resources to provide these and other ministries but also to do them with high quality. As a result, they attract more people, generate even more resources, and enable the church to grow still larger. Many large churches have reached their size at the expense of smaller churches around them, which have been unable to compete.

One thing a large church can't do, however, is be a small church. Large churches can provide small group settings for relationship building, but that's not the same. Small churches come together and stay together out of a sense of belonging and control. A small church is "home" in a way that a large church seldom is. In small churches, family relationships often dominate. It is easier for everyone to feel needed and be important in a smaller church. Consequently, small churches will never disappear. They will, however, be buffeted by competition from larger congregations.

What is a large church? Any congregation that has a year-round average worship attendance of 250 or more is in the top 5 percent of all churches in the United States. Churches averaging 200 and more are well positioned to flourish unless they adopt an exclusive small church mentality that excludes newcomers, restricts ministry and power to old-timers, and fails to effectively minister to people.

Consider this example: The typical locally owned hardware store has less than 5,000 square feet of retail space, whereas the huge Home Depot chain boasts 100,000-plus square feet per store. The local store operates on a limited budget, whereas Home Depot has revenues in the billions of dollars. The local owner has one to three employees, whereas Home Depot has a national staff of more than 100,000. Doesn't seem fair, does it? Read on:

> Ask 43-year-old Dan Hron what he thinks about category-killer Home Depot opening a store half a mile from the tiny hardware store where he's worked nearly 30 years, and he answers:
> "I'm happy."
> That's because Hron expanded his product line, ordered special parts for items that Home Depot sells, and negotiated a service contract to repair the superstore's equipment such as lawn mowers and chainsaws that customers have returned.
> Hron . . . spent a year preparing his store, Johnson

Hardware, for Home Depot's . . . debut . . . which explains
why he is happy. But small hardware store owners who are
not as well prepared can't share Hron's feeling of security.[17]

Leadership in the competitive hardware industry is not too
much different from leadership in the competitive church
world. Leaders of very small churches are probably safe for the
time being because of intense member loyalty. The smallest
churches will live until the last family dies. It is the midsize
churches that are at risk, especially when they are on the way
down. To provide a spiritual home for people who would otherwise be attracted to larger congregations, these churches and
their leaders must have a clear sense of their call from God and
their identity in the community.

One of the ironies is that the midsize church that ministers
effectively will probably grow until it is no longer a midsize
church.

Is Competition Christian?

The church is in competition with a much longer list of
competitors than mentioned here. We are in a culture that is
based on free-enterprise broad competition everywhere in almost everything. We have thousands of people, businesses, bill-
boards, advertisements, and organizations screaming for our
time, money, attention, and loyalty. The competition is so great
that everyone is trying to yell louder and turn up the brightness
of their lights to get our attention. It is either overwhelming or
ignored.

Something about Christianity and the church is so profoundly different that we think we shouldn't compete. In fact,
this is the approach of many church leaders. They refuse to
compete. Some refuse out of frustration; they are paralyzed by
the magnitude of the task. Some refuse out of failure; they tried
once and aren't going to risk it again. Some refuse out of faith,
saying that it's God's responsibility, not theirs.

Let's be both honest and biblical.

When the people of Israel were enslaved in Egypt, there was
competition between the powers of Pharaoh's court magicians
and Moses. Moses operated with God's words, wisdom, and

power. He competed and won. He was a leader and did what a leader needed to do. When the people entered the Promised Land they faced widespread polytheism. In modern terms, we think of conflict between ancient armies. In ancient terms, it was competition between different gods. Yahweh was ready and willing to compete with any of the Canaanite deities. Nation against nation and gods against God, Israel and Yahweh prevailed. Sometimes the competition was amazingly clear-cut, as when Elijah publicly competed against the priests of Baal until they were all defeated.

Not only is competition normal, but leaders who have the knowledge and ability to compete are necessary. One of the primary tasks of a leader is to help others make the right choices in the face of competition. Whether on battlefields or in prayer closets, leaders are needed who can choose between right and wrong and distinguish between better and best.

Chapter 8

Expectations—The Rules Are Changing

WHEN I WAS ASKED to speak to a group of magazine editors about the greatest changes facing church leaders at the turn of the century, I conducted my own survey. Over a period of weeks I interviewed clergy and layleaders from across the country and from a variety of denominational traditions. High on their list of changes was "expectations." Much more is expected of leaders today than a generation ago, they insisted.

Maybe our perceptions are wrong. Maybe the expectations of a previous generation were great and we have forgotten. Maybe we just assume that everything is harder for us than for those who preceded us. But maybe those I interviewed are right.

Many church leaders feel as if they're in a game in which the rules keep changing. Depending on whose rule book they read, the regulations may require traditional music or contemporary music, formal dress or casual dress, male leadership or female leadership, hierarchical structure or flat structure, church growth or church health, small church culture or megachurch culture, denominational affiliations or independent connections, biblical theology or systematic theology, oratorical preaching or conversational preaching, exegetical sermons or narrative sermons.

Many of the expectations differ among generations. Younger church leaders may embrace every new idea that comes along because they want to be on the "cutting edge." They may discount all tradition and believe they are wiser and more competent than those who went before them. Some of these inexperienced leaders have some shocks in store for them. They will discover that the cutting edge is a painful place to be when you're on the wrong side of it. Others will grab the latest fad and hold onto it for the rest of their lives, thus becoming "yesterday's leaders" soon to be criticized by tomorrow's leaders.

At the other extreme are older, more experienced leaders who are unable or unwilling to learn new rules or adapt to new realities. They insist that the old ways were better and may even belittle anything new or different. Their cutting remarks about modern music seem clever to them, but they offend and alienate others. By wishing for the good old days, they guarantee that their wishes will never come true. They are reluctant to learn or read anything new, reluctant to change, and reluctant to believe that God can bless the future in ways other than he blessed the past.

Yes, much is expected of today's leaders, and not only in the church. Almost every area of life has increased expectations for leaders, which is one of the reasons people criticize leaders rather than become leaders. We expect more of politicians, teachers, physicians, condominium association directors, parents, counselors, managers, police officers, and almost everyone else. The rising expectations of leaders in the church are not due primarily to changes in the church but to changes in culture.

Epidemic of Excellence

One of the greatest legacies passed on to the twenty-first century by the twentieth is an "epidemic of excellence." Some trace the epidemic's beginnings to the influence of the American business consultant Edward Demming, who, in one generation, helped the Japanese change the meaning of the phrase "Made in Japan" from *cheap junk* to *highest quality*. In the 1950s the Japanese were beginning to recover from the devastation of World War II. Toys exported to the United States were inexpensive and of poor quality. The imprint "Made in Japan" was a joke for junk. But by the 1980s an astonishing transformation had taken place. Japan became the second largest economy in the world. Lexus automobiles and Nikon cameras competed with the world-renowned quality of German Mercedes and Leica. Sony became a synonym for the very best in consumer electronics. Japanese cars penetrated (some would say dominated) the North American market during the 1980s because of their superior quality. The value of the yen gained unprecedented strength.

A generation ago you needed to change the oil in your car every 1,000 miles, get an engine tune-up every 5,000 miles, and replace your tires every 10,000 miles. If you took really good care of your car you might be able to stretch its life to 100,000 miles. In the 1970s, most odometers rolled back to zero after 99,999 miles because the manufacturers didn't expect their cars to last that long. Today we expect much more of our cars. Even the least expensive cars usually last more than 100,000 miles if you change the oil every 7,500 miles. Tires should take you a minimum of 40,000 miles, though many are good for 60,000 or more. In cold, snowy climates the numbers didn't matter much because the body rusted away before the engine stopped running. Today there are columns of classified newspaper ads for cars with over 120,000 miles that are selling for thousands of dollars, their bodies still intact. This rise in quality has led to an expectation of excellence. In fact, you could say we're experiencing an epidemic of excellence.

Evidence of Excellence:

- Black and white television . . . color television . . . high definition television
- Record albums . . . cassette tapes . . . compact discs
- Radios . . . portable radios . . . boomboxes . . . Sony Walkmans

- Telephones . . . long distance with operators . . . direct dial . . . touch-tone
- Expensive long distance . . . cheap long distance . . . Internet
- Slide rulers . . . calculators . . . computers . . . personal computers . . . laptops
- X-rays . . . CT scans . . . MRIs . . . open MRIs
- 16MM movies . . . color movies . . . sound movies . . . VCRs . . . camcorders . . . DVDs
- Open windows . . . window air conditioners . . . central AC
- Moveable type . . . linotype . . . offset printing . . . desktop publishing
- Carbon copies . . . Mimeograph . . . photocopies
- Eyeglasses . . . contact lenses . . . vision correcting surgery
- Trains . . . propeller planes . . . jet planes . . . jumbo jets . . . supersonic jets
- U.S. mail . . . special delivery . . . FedEx (next day) . . . fax (next minute)
- Cash . . . checks . . . credit cards . . . ATMs and electronic banking
- "Red sky at night, sailor's delight; red sky in morning, sailors take warning" . . . Doppler radar
- Fountain pens . . . ball-point pens . . . felt-tip pens . . . palmtops

We *expect* an immediate answer and courteous service when we call a 1–800 business telephone number (and no more than sixty seconds on hold). We *expect* our cars to be in and out of Jiffy Lube in ten minutes or less. We *expect* the insurance company to pay the claim on time. We *expect* fast food to be hot when served. We *expect* the college placement office to find us a job. We *expect* the snowplow to clear our streets before we have to leave for work in the morning. We *expect* the medicine prescribed by the physician to make us well. We *expect* bottled water to be pure. We *expect* the 9–1–1 call to be instantly answered and the police officers or firefighters to arrive in less than three minutes. We *expect* excellence in education, medicine, government, industry, transportation, banking, sports, construction, communication, and just about everything else.

The epidemic of excellence has not skipped the church or religious organizations. People expect church music to sound as good as the latest CD they bought, the local preacher to be as interesting as the radio preacher, the church newsletter to look as good as the company newsletter, the church building to be as well kept as the school building, church finances to be as carefully handled and reported as the bank's finances, the church secretary to answer the phone as courteously as the customer service representative at the mutual fund company, the climate in the sanctuary to be as comfortable as in the Wal-Mart store, the church sound system to be as clear as the concert hall, and the Sunday school to be as much fun for children as Sesame Street.

Let's not take the time to debate whether or not these are reasonable expectations or even remote possibilities in most churches. The point is that millions of parishioners never consider whether or not they're reasonable. They are so caught up in the epidemic of excellence that anything less stands out as peculiar.

And let's not bother to debate whether these same parishioners live up to standards of excellence themselves. Although it seems fair to expect excellence in attendance, volunteering, giving, loving, learning, worshiping, and everything else Christians are supposed to do, that's not the point either. We are all caught up in the epidemic of excellence, and it does no good to point fingers at each other.

Church leaders are expected to be godly, competent, loyal, effective, articulate, patient, visionary, generous, knowledgeable, loving, and more. The result is that followers are surprised by the absence of excellence but unimpressed with its presence. Consequently, criticism for failure is more common than compliments for success.

This leaves leaders with a sense that nothing will ever be good enough and that the bar is set so high that they will never be able to jump over it. It also leaves them in conflict. After all, excellence is good. No one wants to argue that the ministry of the church and other religious organizations should be shoddy compared to the rest of society.

Does this contribute to a theologically defective culture of performance that bases a person's worth on works rather than on grace? Yes, that is a risk, perhaps even a greater risk now than during some other chapters of history. However, there need not be an essential conflict between grace and excellence. Excellence can and should be undertaken as a service for God.

Conflicting Visions

Many churches have visions that conflict. Some were imported and some are homegrown. Some are spoken and some are assumed. Some are inflexible and some can be changed.

Here is a sample of differing visions in a church of 350 members:

- *Become a megachurch.* Jason and Kim grew up in one of Canada's largest and most successful churches. To them and to their circle of friends, size means success. They want Oaktree Community Church to grow to 1000-plus in average worship attendance, add programs and hire a support staff, begin a television ministry, host large seasonal musical productions, sponsor national conferences of church leaders, and have a senior minister who is a nationally known speaker and author.

- *Become a missions church.* The Great Commission Sunday school class is a group of thirty-five adults who meet faithfully at 9:45 every Sunday morning. They have become close friends. Their passion is missions. Four of the older couples are parents of missionaries serving in Asia and Africa. Two couples are former missionaries themselves. One single woman was a Peace Corps volunteer in Chad (Africa). An orthopedic surgeon in the class is part of a medical practice in which at least one partner spends a month overseas in a missions hospital each year. They spend at least fifteen minutes of every class praying for missionaries, and they are planning to sponsor a "vision tour" to eastern Europe next year. Within the next three years they want the church to be giving 50 percent of its income to missions. They have written a proposal requesting a "missions moment" in every Sunday service and asking that the next new staff member be a missions pastor. Their vision is to be-

come one of the most influential and sacrificial churches in
the United States.

- *Become a caring church.* Betty and Paul are part of one of the
  oldest and largest families in the church. All four of their
  parents were charter members when Oaktree Community
  Church was founded in 1956. The family has had more
  than its share of problems and struggles with four cancer
  deaths within the extended family over the past seven years.
  Add to those tragedies the failure of a family business,
  daughter Jennifer's chronic depression, and son Steve's rejection of the Christian faith and the church. Paul was especially close to the previous pastor, Henry Johnston. They
  grew up together and went to the same schools, and Paul
  was on the search committee that brought Pastor Johnston
  to Oaktree. When he resigned to accept a call to become the
  district superintendent, Paul felt as if he had been permanently removed from the center of church life and influence.
  Betty and Paul are opposed to church growth. They do not
  support or give to missions. As Betty put it, "Why would
  we want more people at Oaktree when we can't care for the
  people we already have? Why should we give half our
  money to missions when we have so many needs right here
  at home?"
- *Become a social concerns church.* The "Compassionate Quartet" is what they have nicknamed themselves, but they are
  really the Social Concerns Committee of Oaktree Church.
  Many are surprised that the four have become such close
  friends. Two grew up with wealth. Two grew up in poverty.
  None of the four volunteered to work on the local Habitat
  for Humanity building project, but all reluctantly agreed
  when they were recruited. That summer they and their
  families worked together on a Habitat house, and it was a
  fabulous experience for all of them. It was especially heart-
  warming when a widow and her four young children moved
  into the completely rebuilt structure. Perhaps most rewarding was their new association with Christians from seven
  other churches who worked on the same house. They talk
  with endless enthusiasm about the ministries of compassion
  flowing from their congregations—feeding the hungry, giv-

ing blood, caring for persons with AIDS, volunteering at a homeless shelter, lobbying the state legislature, running a thrift shop, and financing inner-city enterprises. The Compassionate Quartet wants everyone to share this vision. They dream of the day when the whole church family will care as deeply and work as hard as they do. Imagine the impact of hundreds of church members instead of their small committee. As they often say, "If the pastor would just give his wholehearted support to social ministry, the rest of the church would follow his lead. Without his leadership, it's never going to happen."

- *Become a multi-ethnic church.* The Sparlings know that their vision for Oaktree is not widely held, but they see their vision so clearly and promote it so vigorously that they seem like an army of two. They moved to the area from the San Fernando Valley of Southern California and before that lived on the Hawaiian island of Oahu. They love the multi-cultural, multi-ethnic communities to which they have belonged. To them, the almost-all-white Oaktree Church is boring, maybe even unchristian. They envision a local church that looks and sounds like heaven will someday be—people from every nation, tribe, language, and race. They want the mission statement of the congregation changed to say that "Oaktree Community Church exists to win and gather people of every possible culture and race to live and serve God in Christian harmony and love."

- *Be the way they are.* Last but certainly not least is the group consisting of the Smiths, Johnsons, Hoffmans, Sorentinos, Varigs, Boatmans, Hudsons, MacAndrews, Greeleys, Quinns, Hansens, and most of the other people in Oaktree Church. They like things the way they are. Their vision is to keep the church the way it is. They have worked hard to build the building, support the budget, develop the programs, and get everything the way it is. Their only desire for change is to fine-tune the parts. The Varigs, for example, would like two more members added to the kitchen committee; the Quinns would like the words of hymns printed in the church bulletin instead of just the hymn numbers. But both the Varigs and Quinns are willing to forego these changes lest they unsettle the church in some unexpected way.

That's the short list. Another twenty groups of vocal visionaries could easily be identified. And there may be another twenty groups that are less vocal but see their vision just as clearly and feel just as strongly about it.

In the twenty-first century people will be more educated than any previous generation. They will have traveled to more places, belonged to more churches, lived at more addresses, communicated with more people, and formed more opinions than those living before them.

Nothing is wrong with any of this, but it exponentially raises people's expectations of church leaders. Each special-interest group expects church leaders to see the future the same way the group does. Each expects the leader to turn the group's vision into reality. Each is thrilled when leaders do what the group wants and is disappointed when they don't.

Ironically, leaders who do what a group asks often create dissatisfaction. When the pastor or elders agree with the "caring church crew" and visit their homes and pray with them and give them all the attention they request, they seldom meet the group's expectations. In fact, they're more likely to raise them even higher. The caring crew isn't looking for a one-time expression of pastoral care; they are looking for lifelong attention. When that's not what they get, they become more upset than before because they feel betrayed and abandoned. Their worst fears are realized. Their vision may never come to fruition. So they press even harder to achieve what they believe is best for their church. However, had leaders ignored them, they would have been showing lack of compassion and playing into their accusation that leaders merely use them to fulfill their own agenda.

Enough said. You get the picture. Multiple, often conflicting, visions within the same church complicate the leader's task.

Emerging Expectations

The new rules of church leadership are not available in any list. Like everything else, they are continually changing. But here are some examples that help to explain the changes in leadership expectations. In some instances, the rules for tomorrow are a resuscitation of rules from yesterday.

> Old rule: Faithfulness is sufficient.
> New rule: Effectiveness is expected.

Listen to leaders born before 1950 when they honor individuals retiring from ministry. The most common praise given is for their "faithfulness." Faithfulness means loyalty, showing up, working hard, not complaining, and tolerating less-than-the-best pay and working conditions.

Listen to leaders born after 1950 and the praise you'll hear is for "effectiveness."

The rules have changed. Faithfulness used to be sufficient. Now effectiveness is expected.

This is not to say that an earlier generation rewarded incompetence, nor that today's leaders need not be faithful. It is to say that the pendulum has swung toward an expectation that leaders will not only show up but also know what to do when they get there and get it done before they leave. If they are ineffective, they are more likely to be terminated than they would have been a generation earlier.

The problem arises when a veteran leader is asked to step aside for not doing a good enough job. His response? "But I've worked here for over twenty years. I took a pay cut when the budget was short. I've given my life to this organization." He is explaining why he should stay under the old rules, not realizing that those rules may no longer apply. The new rules ask, "What have you done lately that has made a difference for good?"

> Old rule: Godliness is assumed but not required.
> New rule: Godliness is required but not assumed.

Not too long ago, pastors were assumed to be godly. If a person graduated from seminary and was ordained to the ministry, surely that person must be godly. As long as the pastor carried out the duties of preaching, visiting, marrying, burying, and pastoral care, and didn't do anything bizarre, he was considered a good pastor. Then came the blockbuster revelations of moral failure and financial impropriety among many high-visibility religious leaders during the 1980s and 1990s.

Churches and religious organizations moved godliness to the top of the list of leadership qualifications and increased diligence in determining leaders' character and spirituality. In some cases, would-be leaders are assumed to be less than godly until proven otherwise. The leader is expected to have a close personal relationship with God that is lived out in prayer, chastity, financial accountability, integrity, and relational authenticity. When a flaw is detected, followers are slower to give the leader the benefit of the doubt.

The new rules apply to more than religious leaders. Police officers are screened for use of illegal drugs. Preschool teachers must have annual police background checks. Employers are verifying all academic records listed on a résumé. Search committees are asking pastoral candidates about their sexual morality, prayer and Bible reading habits, sermon study habits, and doctrinal idiosyncrasies. A pastoral search committee in the Pacific Northwest required a candidate to submit his checkbook log for review by a Certified Public Accountant. It is no longer assumed that a person is godly because he or she is a minister. It is no longer assumed that lifelong church membership qualifies a layperson to serve on the church board.

> Old rule: Pastors are "prepared" for ministry.
> New rule: Pastors are lifelong learners.

This rule change applies to nearly every person in every area of life. Training to fly a DC–3 doesn't qualify a person to fly a Boeing 747. Computer skills learned on an Apple IIE do not equip a person to run the latest PC laptop. Graduation from medical school in 1967 may mean that a physician can write "M.D." after her name but does not mean that you want her operating on your son. In each of these cases and a million more, it is necessary to be a lifelong learner.

The church leader who lives by the old rules assumes that degrees, experience, and past successes are all that are needed to lead today's church. Most of the time this is wrong. In fact, yesterday's experiences and successes may be the greatest liability a leader brings to today's opportunities.

Old rule: Reason is more important than relationships.
New rule: Relationships are more important than reason.

Most of the twentieth century could be characterized as a modern age of reason. The scientific method, deductive reasoning, and rationalistic approaches to problems dominated the culture. We liked leaders who were smart and who had all the answers. Following the culture, the church debated the existence of God, published shelves of books defending and explaining Christian teachings, and focused heavily on the advancement of knowledge through church classes. Often, the larger the church, the greater the emphasis on reason.

Reason is still important. Intellectual credibility still holds high value both in society and in religion. However, the importance of relationships has skyrocketed. Today's leaders must be higher in relational skills than in rational skills. Getting along with people is a premium. Church leaders who are alienating, insensitive, distant, unfriendly, or who exhibit other poor social skills usually do not remain long in their leadership positions.

Old rule: The center of influence is the denomination and
            the seminary.
New rule: The center of influence is the large church and
            seminars.

Although this is a change in emphasis rather than a reversal, it is such a profound change that denominational leaders who miss it risk total malfunction in their leadership roles.

Newcomers to a community used to choose a church by its denominational label. Lutherans who were new in a neighborhood always went to the local Lutheran church. Location was important but always secondary to denomination.

This loyalty gave great power to the denomination. Denominational officials considered each local congregation to be a branch office of their church. The denomination wrote the curriculum, appointed the clergy, chose the missionaries, owned the building, provided clergy credentials, set the rules, and took in a percentage of the offerings. Annual denominational budgets were set without a lot of consideration about churches' ability to pay. Churches were expected to pay. If the money didn't come in, churches were assumed to be at fault.

Denominations requiring seminary education for ordination held a monopoly on the clergy socialization process. For three or four years the future ministers were educated by academics (rather than by practitioners) who emphasized scholarly rather than pastoral skills. When pastors needed advice, they called their seminary professors or read books being written by the seminary faculty.

Elements of these old rules remain, more in some traditions than in others. However, big-time changes have come with the new rules. Denominations that take ministry funds from churches are viewed as heavy handed, and an adversarial relationship has developed. The assumption now is that denominations exist to serve the local church rather than the other way around.

Where do church leaders look for examples of how to do church? Increasingly they look to large churches in their own denomination and beyond. These churches are well known, frequently studied, and have become the pacesetters for everything from preaching to music to programs. At the same time, more than three thousand clergy seminars are being offered across the country each year. More are sponsored by megachurches, parachurch organizations, consultants, and other organizations than by seminaries or denominations. They are accessible, affordable, practical, and enormously influential.

> Old rule: Preaching is more important and programs are
>   less important.
> New rule: Programs are more important and preaching is
>   less important.

This rule change is one of the most difficult to understand. The difference is not the decreased importance of preaching but the enormously increased importance of programs.

Preaching used to be the primary attraction to a church and the main function of a minister. The idea that the sermon is 100 percent of the job became the basis for the joke about pastors only working one day a week. It's also why churches became known by the minister's name (e.g., "That's Pastor Brown's church").

Preaching today is like being quarterback on an NFL football team. A team without a good quarterback has little chance of winning. However, it would be a gross misjudgment of the game to think that even the greatest quarterback can carry a weak team to victory. Among the reasons is that the quarterback is only on the field part of the time. The pastor, likewise, depends on other team members for support and also watches from the sidelines much of the time while teammates take their turn on the field.

Music, education, social events, pastoral care, youth ministry, child care, sports, evangelism, discipleship, finances, and facilities are a few of the "special teams" the preacher relies on for support and success. Quality programs are becoming so important that they may be able to carry a weak preacher, but there is no way that a strong preacher can carry weak programming. People choose churches and stay there for many more reasons than in the past. Most of those reasons are spread over the church programs.

> Old rule: Ministry depends on the leader.
> New rule: Ministry depends on the team.

Due to the increased complexity of life in the twenty-first century, no one person is able to do it all; it takes a team to build a church.

Evidence of this rule change can be seen in many quarters, including church planting. For a very long time the only approach used to start new churches was to send a solo pastor into a new community to get a church started. Since 60 percent of new churches close within five years, however, new approaches obviously are needed. One of the more strategic new approaches is to begin with a ministry team that typically includes one full-time pastor, an administrative assistant, a music director, and a children's ministry director. Usually the latter positions are part time. Sometimes there is a second full-time pastor who specializes in music, outreach, or youth ministry. Although this is much more expensive in the beginning, if it significantly increases long-term success, it will be less expensive in the long run.

Another evidence of the rule change is what happens when

a senior minister resigns from a multiple staff church. Some denominations still insist on playing by yesterday's rules, requiring that all other staff also resign to give the new minister a "clean slate." Rather than helping the new pastor, it actually handicaps him because the departing staff members take so much infrastructure, so many relationships, and so much history along with them. Far wiser are those who recognize the value of the rest of the team and hold on to them at least through the first year or two of transition and then decide who stays and who goes.

Under the old rule the pastor functioned as the prima donna of the church. Other leaders were simply the extension of the pastor. The display of the senior pastor's name on the outside church sign is a strong indication that the church is operating by yesterday's rules. Under the new rule, the prima donna is out and the team recruiter and team builder is in. Blessed is the church with leaders who are adept at recruiting and motivating the very best. They have a strong theology of spiritual gifts based on Ephesians 4:11–12 and 1 Corinthians 12–14 and believe that every Christian has equal worth in the church and that each person has individual but interdependent functions. The leader is more like a coach or an orchestra conductor than a boss or owner or star. This type of leader gets great satisfaction out of the successes of others and doesn't try to make it appear as if he or she is the reason for success.

In smaller churches, a hardworking and committed pastor may still be expected to preach, plan and lead worship, teach confirmation, run the Sunday school, oversee church finances, care for the parsonage and church building, visit the sick and elderly, entertain, and represent the church at community events. But this works only as long as the church stays small and the expectations tilt toward the low side. As the church grows and expectations increase, layleaders and other clergy must share leadership responsibilities.

> Old rule: Success is defined by narrow comparison.
> New rule: Success is defined by broad comparison.

Comparisons are common. One of the ways we define ourselves is by comparing ourselves to others. We say we are short because others are taller. We say we are female because others are male. We say we are rich because others have less money. We say we are young because others are older.

Church members have always compared their leaders to other church leaders to determine if what they have is good or bad. However, previous generations had a very limited field of comparison. Most pastors were compared to previous pastors of the same church or pastors of other churches in the same town or pastors of churches where newcomers used to be members. At most, that gave a field of a dozen comparisons, usually less. Because of the limited field of comparison, and because those being compared were often quite similar, everyone looked pretty good.

Under the new rule, the field of comparison is much broader. Because of televised church services, greater travel by church members, increased mobility of members from town to town and church to church, and a wide availability of information about other churches and leaders through tapes, books, and magazines, today's church leaders are compared to hundreds of others. Even more significant is the increased quality of the comparison base. Televised services highlight preachers who are highly skilled communicators from churches famous for their size and success. Many of them write books and magazine articles that increase their visibility, and many of the churches send out books, tapes, videos, and magazines that promote their ministries. The net effect is that the pastor of First Church may be three notches better than the pastor fifty years ago but is rated seven notches lower because of the broad base of comparison with which he competes.

In some ways this seems terribly unfair. No one in First Church is conscious of the comparisons they are making. The rule has changed subtly over a long period of time, raising expectations without most people realizing it.

> Old rule: Credentials are very important.
> New rule: Performance is very important.

In the army everyone knows who is a private, corporal, sergeant, lieutenant, captain, major, colonel, and general. The uniform is one's identity.

In medicine you need certain education plus a license to practice. In construction you have certain training and may have to carry a union card. To teach you need a bachelor's degree and a state license. Credentials are important.

In many denominations clergy positions are open only to those who have met the required educational standards and have been formally ordained. Anyone without credentials is limited, if not excluded, from preaching, serving Communion, conducting weddings, and participating in most other clerical functions. In some traditions ordination brings a "guaranteed call," which means a level of job security whether or not the pastor does the job well. It is similar to faculty tenure, which comes when a teacher has met all the requirements and is granted lifetime appointment unless he or she is found guilty of gross misconduct.

At the other end of the spectrum are denominations that give clergy status to anyone claiming to have heard God's "call to preach." No special education or training is required.

In some situations a denomination's approval is not even necessary. A person can start a church without any education, credentials, or ordination. Once the church is started and legally organized and recognized, it can ordain ministers by whatever rules the founders want to establish.

The extreme differences regarding church credentialing aren't the point here; the point is that the rule change is stretching across all traditions. The old rule is that credentials are very important; without them, people won't follow your leadership. The new rule is that performance is very important; if you do a good job, you'll gather followers regardless of credentials; if you do a poor job, you'll lose followers regardless of credentials.

One of the common evidences of this rule change is the creative ways in which denominational churches are getting around the rules. The Roman Catholic Church is the strictest of all in formal requirements. In order to be a priest you must be male, educated, celibate,[1] and ordained by a bishop. There is a huge shortage of priests in the Roman Catholic churches of North America. In the archdiocese of St. Paul and Minneapolis there are only 246 priests for 720,000 Roman Catholics (i.e., one priest for every 2,927 Roman Catholics). The number of

Catholics is projected to grow by 10,000 per year over the coming decade, while the number of priests is expected to drop below 190.[2] There is a growing need for clergy functions and a growing shortage of priests. Increasingly there are large Catholic churches with thousands of members, one priest, and staffs similar to those in Protestant megachurches. These churches have full-time employees who do pastoral care, youth ministry, visitation, and a whole array of other pastoral functions. In some churches laypreachers deliver homilies, and ordained deacons (who can be married and who often have a second vocation) conduct weddings and funerals. (One exception would be in a service where Mass is celebrated, in which case a priest would have to also be present.)

For Protestant churches this rule change means that traditional churches will find more ways around the credentialing rules to get high-performers into church leadership positions. Seminaries will hire presidents who have law degrees or MBAs but lack theological education. Nondenominational churches may be started by pastors who have no credentials at all except the abilities to preach and lead. Some will become famous for their success. At the other extreme, low performers with lots of credentials will have increased pressure to change or to leave.

Trying Harder Doesn't Always Help

When the rules change, many good people resist and just try harder to succeed under the old rules. In football, this would be like a team refusing to acknowledge the legality of the forward pass and trying to improve their running game. In basketball, this would be like ordering players to hold their shots until they are close to the basket because you dislike the three-point shot. In timekeeping, this compares to leaving your watch on standard time because you don't approve of daylight saving time.

The older we are and the greater our past successes, the less we like change, the more we prefer yesterday over tomorrow, and the harder we try to succeed by the old rules.

Sometimes trying harder helps. Roman Catholics who grieved the loss of the Latin liturgy have revived it with increased excellence. Some churches insist on using language a younger generation doesn't understand, music that no longer connects to the heart, times of services that are inconvenient, clothes that few wear and are difficult to buy, and sermons that answer questions no longer being asked. But they are doing all these things better than ever. The result is a greater and more loyal share of a fast-shrinking market.

Most of the time trying harder doesn't work well. Shouting louder seems strange in an era with public address systems. Bigger fans seem silly at a time when most homes and businesses have central air conditioning. The leader who does everything himself in a context of teams seems greedy, not self-sacrificing. Using academic credentials after the pastor's name seems arrogant at a time when competence and effectiveness are preferred. Talking about a textbook read years ago in college undermines leadership credibility more than it helps, especially when followers would rather know if the leader is reading current books.

Is it hard to lead when expectations are increasing? Is it a challenge to keep up with new expectations when they keep changing? Is it discouraging to feel as if you don't measure up to expectations when you are working so hard to do your best? The same word answers all these questions: Yes. One of the realities of leadership is that the change of millennia on the calendar means a change in expectations for leaders.

Chapter 9

Relationships—It's Who You Know

TWO GENERATIONS of television viewers grew up watching medical shows with physician heroes named Dr. Kildare, Trapper John, Ben Casey, and Marcus Welby, M.D. They were all top-rated programs centered on individuals.

Robert Young played the role of Dr. Marcus Welby, a family physician whose office was in his home. As a general practitioner he was nothing short of amazing. Week after week he performed medical miracles for his patients. It seemed as if there were no illness he could not diagnose, no question he could not answer, no malady he could not cure. Every viewer wanted him for a personal physician. Every medical doctor in America either wanted to be like Dr. Welby or resented the unrealistic standards he set.

In the 1990s television abandoned the hero doctors and created a new top-rated medical show called *ER*. Set in the emergency room of a large Chicago general hospital, the program features stories that do not always end happily. Not every patient is cured. Many die. But the greatest change from the earlier generations of medical TV is the lack of a central hero. *ER* was created as an ensemble show; the characters are a team; no one person is central. Much of the script is about relationships and how those relationships weave into the practice of emergency medicine.

The changed focus of medical television reflects a similar change in the broader culture as heroes disappear and relationships take on greater importance.

"Us" in an Individualistic Culture

All cultures fit someplace on a continuum from the greater importance of the individual to the greater importance of the group. No culture operates completely at either extreme, but some go far in one direction or the other.

Western missionaries have been chagrined by cultures in which every member of a tribe wants to convert to Christianity when the chief or tribal leader does. The missionary may insist, "You can't do that! Christianity is a *personal* faith." To Westerners, group conversion isn't really conversion at all. It's merely going along with everyone else.

Americans tilt toward the other extreme. Even though we come from a broad mix of cultures, we are highly individualistic. One of the reasons may be our genetic history. Most of our foreparents came to this continent by leaving family, friends, and traditions behind. It took courage to move out. Coming to America usually meant starting from scratch with few resources. America may have been the land of opportunity, but it was also the land where only the fittest survived. Whether the newcomers arrived as explorers, pilgrims, refugees, or slaves, they all had to make their own way in a new and challenging land where independence and individualism were life-and-death matters.

As the nation matured and immigrants settled, new neighborhoods were established and extended families grew. Individualism survived, but a sense of community gained strength. The Great Depression seemed to reinforce both individualism and community as the need for individual resourcefulness was matched by the need for neighbors. In the long run, however, individualism prevailed. Survivors of the Depression were left with a lack of trust in banks, businesses, and other failed institutions. The hard lesson they learned was the need to take care of yourself and your own.

World War II brought the nation together around a single cause and ushered in the postwar boom. The economy soared, houses went up, and so did the birthrate as babies were born in record numbers. The good times had come.

Prosperity brought mobility. By 1970 one-fifth of Americans were changing their "permanent address" every calendar year. Employees of the emerging computer giant IBM joked about the letters meaning *"I've Been Moved."* Once again individualism was reinforced as mobile Americans were disconnected from neighborhoods, communities, and extended families. Fewer children grew up near grandparents, aunts, uncles, and cousins.

The Vietnam War and the Watergate crisis added institutional distrust to the cultural mix. Those who opposed the war were young and lacked the fierce nationalism of World War II veterans. The generation that had fought for the American flag had to watch the next generation wear it stitched to their clothes or burned as part of an antigovernment protest. On every side of almost every issue was growing disenchantment with government, education, leaders, and everything institutional. Even the church, marriage, and families came under attack and distrust. It was a difficult and defining time for American culture, and the scars it left formed new patterns in the way people relate. Cynicism soared, and individualism gained more strength.

In many ways, the 1990s, with even more societal changes, made Americans more individualistic, especially in the workplace. Job security decreased, and workers learned to watch out for themselves. No longer could they expect lifelong employment. Loyalty didn't help when the company was sold or merged, resulting in massive layoffs. Most workers today have a series of jobs and multiple careers over a working lifetime. The security of company pensions with defined benefits started to disappear in favor of 401k and 403b defined-contribution plans. Employees were introduced to the importance of individual retirement accounts. The press repeatedly insisted that Social Security wasn't all that secure and that people ought to be planning and providing for themselves.

If the trend of individualism was extrapolated into the future it would end in ultimate isolation—every individual completely disconnected from every other individual. But trends rarely run forever. Culture is like a river that runs high in the spring and dry in the fall. People react. Reversals are common.

While acknowledging that individualism is still a powerful force in American culture, we can't deny that relationships have become increasingly important. Isolated people want to get connected. Children of divorce want lasting marriages. Loners are deciding to become joiners. Yesterday's ambitious executives on the way to the top are deciding to decline lucrative promotions and transfers in order to stay in their neighborhoods and keep family and friendships intact. Companies are building with fewer closed offices and more modular designs; conference areas are popular and frequently used. Baseball, a sport that emphasizes individual skills, is declining in popularity, while soccer, a sport that emphasizes team skills, is increasing.

Even the venerable Pulitzer Prizes are undergoing profound changes. The Pulitzer is the honor given for excellence in journalism. Since 1917 the Pulitzer Board has given most awards to individual journalists. The notable exception was the annual granting of the "public service award" to specific organizations. In 1999 a historic shift occurred. A majority of Pulitzer Prizes went to "collectives"—newspaper and wire service staffs and an editorial board. This is the result of a forty-year trend away from individual awards and toward team awards. According to Philip Meyer of *USA Today*, "Reporting, once a trade for generalists whose main qualifications were energetic curiosity and a talent for writing, has become a mosaic of specialties. The old adage that 'a good reporter is good anywhere' no longer holds. Now it takes a good committee."[1]

Consider what Americans told the Harris Poll about what is most important in life:[2]

- relationships (56%)
- religious faith (21%)
- making the world a better place (12%)
- a fulfilling career (5%)
- money (5%)

Americans count relationships to be more important than money by a margin of more than ten to one. Some may be tempted to say, "But there's a difference between a popular survey and the actual decisions people make when it comes down to a choice between friends and cash." That may be true, but a growing cadre of employers are hearing their employees refuse job transfers and promotions because it would be too disruptive to personal and family relationships.

In another poll, researchers asked Americans age twenty-one and older to identify their "very strong" commitments:[3]

- family (90%)
- relationships/friendships (79%)
- job (54%)
- religion (52%)
- charities/causes (22%)
- political party (18%)

No matter which segment of society we examine, the increased importance of relationships shows up. Gangs have become a major element of the youth and young adult culture of North American cities. Sociologists work hard to understand this social phenomenon, and police departments have special units to try to limit criminal gang activity. Almost everyone will agree that gangs are strong because of the relationships they provide. A gang is a group to belong to, a "family" to count on, a place to find identity. Attempts to break up gangs without substituting other equally viable relationships probably won't work. Gang life extends from the streets to prison and from youth to adulthood. Whether good or bad, gangs are about relationships.

Just as relationships can drag people down, relationships can also teach people what is good. Chuck Colson of Prison Fellowship quoted this from a *Newsweek* magazine article: "An ethics of virtue cannot . . . be taught from textbooks. Good character comes from living in communities—family, neighborhood, religious and civic institutions—where virtue is encouraged and rewarded." Colson added, "That echoes a truth expounded by Aristotle, who said that character is inculcated through community groups that provide models to imitate, that demand moral accountability."[4] In other words, the best channel to develop virtue and good is through community relationships.

I am increasingly convinced that relationships are the primary gateway to evangelism, the church, and ministry. Not that reason is unimportant, but relationships are more important. This became evident in a conversation I had with the local leader of a well-known religious cult. He told me that they expect to get one convert for every one thousand homes when they knock on the doors of strangers. That is a 1:1000 ratio. Then he claimed one convert for every two neighbors who are entertained in the home of a member of his religion. That is a 1:2 ratio. It seemed obvious to me that knocking on doors was a comparative waste of time when they can do far better befriending others in their apartment complex or neighborhood. It also impressed me that their religious beliefs weren't the determining factor in conversions. The determining factor is relationships. If they make friends, they win converts. If they talk to strangers, they get nowhere. It also seemed obvious to me that the principle applies to orthodox Christian churches as well as fringe cult groups. Whoever builds the best relationship is most likely to win a convert.

This is a very important cultural trend that we cannot ignore. But it is not simple. Like most trends affecting leadership in the twenty-first century, this one is mixed. Large percentages of Americans want relationships but don't want to join anything. So while relationships have skyrocketed in importance, membership in political parties has plummeted. Most Americans are now political "independents" rather than declared affiliates of major political parties. The "we want relationships but we don't want to join" attitude also affects community service clubs, parent-teacher organizations, labor unions, and churches. Perhaps the contradiction is most obvious in men and women who desperately desire a meaningful relationship with one another but choose to live together outside of a marital relationship.

Connecting at Church

One young mother came to a Mothers-of-Preschoolers (MOPS) weekday program at Wooddale Church because another mother in her neighborhood invited her. She had no church background and no religious interest. She simply had a friend and wanted to make more friends. MOPS was a positive experience. Her relationships multiplied and deepened. As Christmas neared she saw a poster in the church building advertising the annual Christmas concert. Since she and her husband liked good music, they decided to attend. As they drove home that night they agreed that they had enjoyed the music. They decided that it would be good for them to raise their children in a church, something neither of them experienced growing up. Before they reached home they decided to join Wooddale Church and raise their children there—although they acknowledged to each other that they had no idea as to what kind of church it was or what the church believed and taught. Unusual? Probably not. More and more unbelievers first come to church because of relationships, not religion. They are most likely to adopt the beliefs and faith of their friends.

This has profound implications for how we go about evangelism in the third millennium. We have switched from the old way when people came to church and then made friends to the new way when people make friends and then come to church. If this is so, what are the implications for churches in which all the members are friends with one another but not with outsiders? What happens to the church with so many programs targeting insiders that all available time is consumed going to church events? The answer is obvious—such churches serve themselves, fail to reach outsiders, and do not grow.

Kathy is a good example. She was a successful stockbroker in Minneapolis who easily made friends and had the gift of evangelism. She used to put on her swimsuit, go to the pool at her apartment complex, settle on a chaise lounge, read a book, and eventually strike up a conversation with whoever sat next to her. Soon the two would become friends and Kathy would begin talking very comfortably about her Christian faith. Bringing newcomers to church was her regular practice. She was so good at this that she was invited to serve on the church evangelism board. When Kathy asked me what I thought about the idea I said, "It seems ridiculous. Why would we put someone who is so good at evangelism in a room for hours with people who are already Christians? Let someone else serve on the evangelism board while you sit out by the pool." Get the friendly relational people out of the church building and into the community. Capitalize on the popularity and importance of relationships.

Once people are inside the church, relationships continue to be important. But the patterns often vary with church size and style. Small churches are usually connected through family systems. In an established congregation of fifty or fewer, bloodlines are the glue holding the people together. This is both an asset and a liability. The asset is that small churches can be almost indestructible—burn down the building, fire the pastor, get excommunicated from the denomination, and bankrupt the corporation, but services will still be held next Sunday. When everyone is related, such things don't matter much. This church can meet in someone's living room. The liability is that outsiders have trouble getting inside. Even pastors may never really be accepted. The pastor can serve the congregation for twenty-five years and still be an outsider because he has no blood relationship in the church. "Chaplain," maybe; but "pastor," probably never.

Shortly after graduating from seminary I told a friend from Maine that I would love to pastor a country church in his state. I had only visited there, so I did not understand what he knew. Sensing his unease, I asked him if he thought I would ever be accepted there. Simply but deliberately he said, "No." Then I asked, "If our children were born there would they be accepted?" He said, "We have a saying in Maine: 'If a cat has its kittens in the oven, does that make them biscuits?' " I went to Colorado.

Recognizing the enormous importance of relationships and relational structures is essential for leaders in every church. To assume that all churches are the same and that relationships do not differ from place to place and from church to church is leadership suicide.

The same principle applies in a different way in large churches—those with a yearly average worship attendance of 250, or more. This is a comparatively elite group, since only the largest 5 percent of all North American congregations fall into this category. These are multiple-cell congregations in which not everyone knows everyone else on a first-name basis. People are closely connected to a few and loosely connected to everyone else. These churches are much easier for outsiders to penetrate and much easier for newcomers to find friends. However, they are challenging to lead. Every subgroup is different. The leader must learn how the groups are populated and organized and how to relate differently to each. Not everyone can be treated and led in the same way. Old-timers are led with knowledge of their history and respect for their traditions. Newcomers are led with respect for their needs and understanding of their reasons for coming. Specialists are led by understanding and relating to their special interests such as music, missions, social action, child care, or sports. Inactive members are led by understanding their desire to remain affiliated without feeling connected. Founders are led by listening to their original vision and translating that vision into present and future goals. All of these different groups are connected to the church through intricate and overlapping webs of relationships that comprise the social and spiritual fabric of the congregation.

During a recent regional conference in southern Illinois I was explaining these concepts to the leaders of churches from Illinois and Missouri. I suggested that they map the relationships of their churches, seeking to identify the various groups in the church and how they connect to the congregation. Specifically, I suggested that the leaders of each church discuss this until they were able to draw the relational organization of the church on a piece of paper and agree that "this is the way the church relates and works." That was on a Friday evening. Before the next session on Saturday morning a group of six leaders from one church came and said to me, "We followed your suggestion. We went out to a restaurant after last night's session and started talking about the various relational groups in our church. Then we turned over our paper place mats and started drawing. We kept talking and drawing and talking and drawing until we stayed up all night in that restaurant, ate breakfast, and came directly to this morning's session." Then they added the best line of all: "Even though some of us have been in the church for years, this is the first time we have understood this congregation and known how to lead it."

Leaders who don't understand and use the relational map of the church or organization they lead are like travelers trying to find their way through an unfamiliar city without a map or directions.

The importance of relationships to the life of the Christian community is no modern concept. It is deeply rooted in the New Testament concept of the church. The Great Commission assumes that evangelism comes out of relationships: "Therefore go and make disciples of all nations, baptizing them in the name of the Father and of the Son and of the Holy Spirit, and teaching them to obey everything I have commanded you. And surely I am with you always, to the very end of the age" (Matthew 28:19–20). The "you" in this mandate is plural. It would be impossible and discouraging to think that the call to disciple all nations (people from Jerusalem, Judea, Samaria, *and* the rest of the world, according to Acts 1:8) is an individual, personal responsibility. The call of Jesus and the best methodology for evangelization is through teams of Christians working together.

This principle has not always been recognized by mission agencies. In the past, individual missionaries or missionary couples were sent to distant cities to win converts and establish beachhead churches. The result often was ineffectiveness and excessive missionary casualties. Most mission organizations now send teams of individuals and couples, recognizing that multiple people means multiplied encouragement, which results in multiplied effectiveness. To a lesser extent the team concept is being practiced in North American church planting efforts. (See chapter 8.)

- The "one another" theme of the first-century church is woven throughout the New Testament. Fifty-eight times in fifty-six verses Christians are connected to "one another" relationally. In light of this frequency, we can assume that interpersonal connections are a theological priority as well as a sociological necessity.
- Spiritual gift theology is introduced in 1 Corinthians 12–14 and expanded in Ephesians 4 and 1 Peter 4. After listing many of the gifts, the apostle Paul writes, "All these are the

work of one and the same Spirit, and he gives them to each one, just as he determines. The body is a unit, though it is made up of many parts; and though all its parts are many, they form one body. So it is with Christ" (1 Corinthians 12:11–12). Spiritual gift theology precludes "lone ranger" Christians who operate independently of other believers. It is as absurd as an eye or an ear trying to operate independently of the rest of a human body.

The impact of relationships on modern churches is seen in the movement away from traditional governance structures and toward ministry teams. In traditional structures, the denomination oversees the church, the church oversees the board, the board oversees committees, and committees oversee volunteers. In many ways it is a system based on lack of trust and the assumption that everyone needs to be watched and supervised. Too often the people being supervised know more about the ministry than those who are supervising them. Ministry is mistakenly defined as going to meetings to talk about other people doing ministry.

In contrast, many new churches are organizing around ministry teams, and many established churches are abandoning traditional structures and adopting a ministry team approach.

Ministry teams vary from church to church but are typically like self-directed work groups in businesses. The team is comprised of the people who do the ministry. They make their own decisions and develop their own goals in accordance with the overall rules and structures of the church. The teams may minister in areas of music, children's education, evangelism, stewardship, discipleship, or any other church function. They are organized to get the job done. People on the teams become friends around common goals, and the mix of work and relationships is energizing, not exhausting. They connect to church leaders for empowerment, not supervision. The role of the church leader is to help ministry teams succeed. This is very much in keeping with the teaching of Ephesians 4:12, which says leadership gifts are to be used "to prepare God's people for works of service, so that the body of Christ may be built up."

Recruiting and Retaining Volunteers

Leaders are often recruiters. Understanding and following the relational rules for recruiting and retaining volunteers significantly multiplies the effectiveness of leadership in churches and other volunteer organizations.

Peter Drucker says that every second American adult serves as a volunteer in America's nonprofit sector, averaging at least three hours a week. This makes nonprofits America's largest employer.[5] Gallup reports that in 1995, 93 million Americans were volunteers, each averaging 218 hours per year. In addition to adults, 13 million teen volunteers (ages 12–17) averaged 182 hours each per year.[6] We are a nation of volunteers. Americans have a predisposition to help out. This makes the leader's task easier, but there are some important relational rules the leader needs to know and follow:

Rule #1—Begin with the person. Most new volunteers don't have a significant commitment to the organization or task. They are interested in their own issues and needs because that's what they know.

Jesus always began with the needs of others. Sometimes the need was food, sometimes health, sometimes family, sometimes answers to questions. Jesus met people's needs before expecting them to move to where they needed to be.

Unfortunately, many of those who recruit volunteers focus on the job they want done.

A professional fund-raiser once told me, "I never begin with their money or our need. I always begin with the person." His goal, he says, is to help the donor meet her needs through giving. If her needs do not match his organization, he considers it a matter of personal integrity to say so and move on.

An old communication adage reminds us of this: "An amateur asks, 'What should I say?' A professional asks, 'Who is my audience?' " Beginning with the other person always means listening before speaking, finding out what others need before saying what you need. The best leaders don't have to fake this interest; they don't play with people's emotions for their own selfish purposes. The best leaders begin with the other person because they care about other people.

Rule #2—Ask. The number-one reason people volunteer is because they are asked. Only 21 percent of adults volunteer without being asked; 85 percent volunteer when they are asked. When talking to teen volunteers ages twelve to seventeen, the number jumps to an amazing 93 percent who volunteer when they are asked.[7]

Studies conducted by *U.S. News & World Report* and the Pew Research Center indicate that there are 72 million Americans who don't currently volunteer. Perhaps it's because no one has ever asked them. If 85 percent of nonvolunteers were asked and said yes, we would have another 61 million volunteers in America.

The way we ask is important. A common strategy is to use guilt as a motivator. One of the reasons we use it is because it works so well. We say things like, "If you won't do this, no one else will"; and, "A lot of children are going to suffer the rest of their lives if you don't help them." One problem with motivation by guilt is that it only works for the short term. Guilt often turns to resentment toward those who did the recruiting and then toward the organization they represent.

Consider two superior motivators:

- *Gratitude*—Encourage potential volunteers to reflect on all that is good in their lives and express their gratitude to God by sharing some of their blessings with others.
- *Discontent*—Find out what it is that a person wants to change in his or her life. Truly content people never do anything; they like everything the way it is. It is only when we are dissatisfied with the way things are that we are willing to take action to change them. The good news is, there is plenty of discontent in our world and therefore plenty of motivation for action. The recruiter who asks a volunteer to do something that will bring the person satisfaction will get a good response that has a high probability of lasting for a long time.

Rule #3—Combine high expectations with strong enabling. Volunteers of whom little is expected probably will make minimal contribution and soon quit. There is little satisfaction in doing something below your potential that doesn't make much difference. Why bother?

In contrast, imagine being asked to do something big and important that will stretch and challenge you. Nonprofit organizations that expect a lot from their donors and volunteers get a lot in return. Those that expect little usually get little.

However, high expectations alone can be disastrous. If I am expected to do something stretching and significant but fail, I will feel bad about myself and be reluctant to volunteer again. No one wants to fail.

The best organizations provide strong support and enabling to go along with the high expectations. When a volunteer agrees to accept challenges beyond his experience and receives help in achieving them, he will feel good about the leader who recruited him, the organization, and himself. That motivates him to volunteer again and to try something even more challenging. When you keep raising the standard and keep helping volunteers reach it, you create synergy that fuels future endeavors.

Rule #4—Volunteers must be paid. This rule seems obviously wrong. Actually, it is obviously right. Volunteers must be paid, just like employees. The difference is that they are not paid with money; they are paid with intangible but very real rewards.

Volunteers must get as much (or more) out of their volunteering as they are putting into it. Otherwise, they will quit.

In a speech given to a management conference, David Hubbard, then president of Fuller Theological Seminary, said that every board member must get more than he or she gives. Every board meeting must have in-service training, networking, challenging opportunities, and significantly satisfying experiences.

The realization of this rule is read in almost every newspaper article telling the story of a volunteer. Frequently the volunteer is quoted as saying, "I get more out of this than I put into it." Whether tutoring a child, building dikes against a flood, teaching Sunday school, or giving a one million dollar gift—the volunteer should always sense that the satisfaction received is as great or greater than the service or gift given.

Leaders of churches and Christian organizations should think through how much their board members are being paid with nonmonetary rewards. Those with strong boards demonstrating great loyalty and making significant contributions are probably paying them well. If there is a frequent turnover of board members and other volunteers, if meetings are missed and assignments are ignored, the members probably are being underpaid or unpaid.

Several years ago the chairman of the Wooddale Church elder board distributed sheets of paper listing every board member's name and the names of immediate family members. He called each elder by name, looked each one in the eye, and said, "I promise to pray every day for you, your spouse, and your children—by name." Then he asked each of the rest of us to make the same promise to the others in the room. One by one, each of us promised to pray daily, by name, for each elder and each elder's family members. The board experienced wonderful solidarity, rare absences, long-term commitment, unanimity, and effectiveness. Where else can you get this kind of promise? Where else can you receive this level of personal support? Where else can you get someone to pray for those you love the most? We were all very well paid!

The Relational Leader

If the leader understands and leverages relationships, the outcome will be exponentially better than if the leader doesn't. But what does this mean?

A rough rule of thumb has been true in most churches over recent generations. It states that "the smaller the church, the greater the importance of relationships; the larger the church, the greater the importance of performance." In an oversimplified illustration, a soloist in a small church will be well received if everyone knows and likes her even though she mumbles her words and misses most of her notes. The soloist in the large church will be well received if she sings the words clearly and hits all her notes even though she has a less than pleasant personality.

Of course it's never quite that simple. Really bad music is pretty hard to hear even if the soloist is your best friend. And really good music is tough to take when you don't like the person who is singing. But the gap is closing. Musical excellence is so common that poor quality is less tolerable in even the smallest and most relational family churches. And people with irritating personalities are less often allowed to minister even if they are highly gifted musicians. Higher expectations on performance. Higher expectations on relationships.

The effective leader understands how people connect with one another. The effective leader cares about people and enables them to find satisfying relationships within the church. The effective leader never ignores the importance of relationships for the sake of accomplishing a task.

Chapter 10

Stress—The Weight That Holds Us Down

WHAT DOES STRESS feel like? It feels like constant pressure. It feels like being trapped. It feels like having more to do than I can ever get done. It feels like other people and circumstances have taken control of my life. For the most part, it doesn't feel very good.

Whose fault is it? My quick response is to say that none of it is my fault. I didn't invent the seven-day week with fifty-two Sundays a year (I have often wished for a metric week with Sundays coming every ten days instead of every seven).

But the truth is, I am far more responsible for my situation than I want to admit.

When the pastor of a 700-member East Coast church called me, he sounded as if he was ready to crack. He asked if I had a few minutes to talk, but for the next hour he did most of the talking. He recited all the things he had to do, places he had to go, and people he had to serve. He reported a long list of criticisms from people in his church—criticisms that hurt him and made him feel unappreciated and betrayed by those he was pouring out his life to serve. He was working 80–100 hours each week, but when he told the board members of the church his litany of complaints at the previous night's board meeting, they didn't do anything to solve the problems. He wanted my advice about what to do.

He asked for my opinion, so I gave it. I told him that I thought most of the stress was his responsibility, a result of his choices, and inside his head more than in his circumstances. While there were many ways the church could help him (he had suggested that they hire a new assistant pastor—which may or may not lower his stress), most of the resolution would have to come from him. He would have to decide what to do and what not to do. He would have to set his own boundaries and determine his own perspective on everything from workload to criticism. No one else can relieve his stress load if he insists on creating new stresses.

So is it his fault? Yes and no. The majority of stress factors are under the leader's control, but there are many external factors that cause it. Unfortunately, we are beginning the new century with increased causes for stress and decreased skills with which to resolve and manage them.

Stressors

"Stressor" is a new word; it's not in every dictionary. But we all know what the word means. Stressors are the things that cause stress in our lives. My dictionary defines "stress" as "strain or straining force; specif., (a) force exerted upon a body, that tends to strain or deform its shape. . . ."[1]

In other words, stressors are the external forces that put pressure on our lives. They are real and they are powerful.

Tough at the top

To be candid, the stress of being the top leader of any organization cannot be easily understood by anyone who does not hold such a position. It is part of the loneliness of leadership.

The *Wall Street Journal* ran a front-page feature story about the stresses common to the chief executive officers of major businesses:

> Midway through another 14-hour day, depleted after six meetings, an employee pep rally, eight stock price updates and more than a dozen expletives, Allan Schuman rubs his eyes.
>
> "My wife says to me, 'This is crazy! You're the CEO. You're in charge. Why do you work so hard?' " says the 64-year-old Mr. Schuman, who heads Ecolab Inc., a $1.9 billion maker of commercial cleaning supplies. "But you're constantly pushing. It never ends. You can never let up."
>
> The grueling workplace has reached the top floor. Not so long ago, being chief executive officer often meant being principal business strategist and corporate ambassador to the outside world. These days, amid the uncertainties created by globalization and rapid technological change, CEOs are expected to be hands on managers. And those who don't manage to deliver growth and higher stock prices often face the ax.[2]

Especially interesting to me were the comments of David Wessner, CEO of HealthSystem Minnesota. He had grown up in the home of a leader because his father was the CEO of ServiceMaster Company. Yet Wessner, when he became a CEO himself, "was 'overwhelmed' by the 'complete focus it required, the expectations that came from outside and inside the organization, the great discipline it required of time and energy.' He says he has adjusted, but the job has created 'stress for my family.' "[3]

When pastors from across America entered the auditorium at a national conference, one of the first sights they saw was a large banner above the platform that said, "Relax. You're not responsible." It probably made them feel good, because most top leaders feel responsible for their organizations and the people in them most of the time. It is a twenty-four-hours-a-day, 365-days-a-year responsibility.

Finances

One stress factor faced by many leaders of churches and Christian organizations that is not faced by CEOs of multibillion dollar corporations is low salaries.

Most, however, do not complain. Surveys of American

pastors indicate that they earn less, give more, and owe less than most others in the country. It's not because they are superior money managers but because they choose to live out and model biblical principles of contentment, stewardship, and generosity. They certainly recognize and admit to financial struggles but consider the privileges of ministry to outweigh the hassles with money.[4]

Most vocational Christian leaders are underpaid considering their education, experience, and responsibility. Although most don't complain, the economic pressure adds stress to their lives. The immediate stress comes from day-to-day expenses. At one point in my pastoral experience every credit card was at the limit, we were making the minimum payment every month, and I didn't have a dollar in my wallet. It was a memorably painful day when our young children wanted to stop at McDonald's on the way home from a church service and I didn't have enough money for us to eat there.

The potential for stress increases when other financial factors are added in: paying off long-term education loans, maintaining a standard of living comparable to others in the community while receiving lower compensation, building an emergency savings fund, preparing for retirement.

There is a difference between greedy self-advancement and financial health. When there is never enough money, the shortage can leak like a poison into every other area of life. Parenting, pastoring, planning, and even playing can become stressful due to financial problems.

Work load

During the 1960s colleges offered courses in the sociology of leisure on the premise that the American workweek would get shorter and shorter. Some predicted that leisure would be the largest American industry by the end of the twentieth century because the average workweek would be less than thirty hours. They were very wrong. The workweek is getting longer, not shorter. More members of each household are in the work force. Commute times are growing longer. We're tired . . . and stressed.

Richard Swenson, M.D., the director of the Future Health Study Center in Menomonie, Wisconsin,[5] is a reservoir of relevant and interesting statistics:

- The average desk workers have thirty-six hours of work on their desks and spend three hours a week sorting the piles.
- Fifty percent of managers say the uncontrolled flood of information constitutes a major stressor in the workplace every day; 95 percent say it won't improve.
- "Moonlighting" and overtime in America are at record levels.
- Men are averaging forty-seven hours a week at work. Two-thirds of married women working outside the home are working sixty-five to eighty-five hours a week when combined with domestic work hours at home.
- American workers put in more hours on the job than workers in any other industrialized country surveyed, averaging 280 more hours a year than the Germans.
- It takes twenty to thirty phone calls in the average church today to get the same number of volunteers it used to take two to three phone calls to get.
- One missions executive said, "We are now getting missionary candidates beginning their careers burned-out." Ninety percent of pastors say they are inadequately trained to cope with ministry demands.[6]

Ninety percent of pastors work more than forty hours per week and many often work more than sixty.[7]

At the same time, layleaders of churches are working forty to sixty hours per week on their jobs plus volunteering ten to twenty hours per week as church leaders. Often there is minimal understanding of the others' work, fatigue, or stress.

Stress epidemic

A major stressor is the stress epidemic. Stress seems to be everywhere and growing. Anyone who spends much time around stressed-out people knows how stressful that can be. We are compounding one another's stress.

Richard Swenson says, "When we cross the threshold of our

limits and become saturated with overload, we begin to resent the very things we once desired to do. Pastors begin to resent their parishioners for having problems and needs."[8]

To slow down in a culture that is speeding up is very difficult to do. It appears to be laziness or selfishness (and sometimes it is). However, if leaders won't or can't set an example contrary to the negative aspects of the trend, who will? How the leader copes will become the model for followers.

Personal problems

Leaders are people with the same sicknesses, sins, and struggles as everyone else. None of us has the whole catalog of issues, but none of us is exempt from such problems as physical weakness, fatigue, interpersonal conflicts, marriage differences, prodigal children, lust, anger, sensitivity to criticism, theological doubts, or emotional dysfunction.

Frankly, these can be much harder to deal with if you are a leader. On one extreme are those who insist that transparency and vulnerability are always good—show your followers that you are as human as they are. That advice may be okay if it is just you, but when your revelation of pain requires an announcement about your spouse's mental illness, your daughter's promiscuity, or your son's drug abuse, it may not be okay. In the name of transparency, you may do severe damage to a family member who is powerless to stop your revelations. At the other extreme is secrecy that refuses to tell anyone anything. With that secrecy can come an overwhelming sense of isolation, guilt, and loneliness. Besides, those who keep secrets often learn that they lack the outside help they desperately need and end up having their secrets told by others.

I have no prescription that works in every situation. But I do know that the leader's personal problems can make other stresses greater. It is hard to go away on a business trip when things are not right at home. It is difficult to preach on a Sunday morning when you've been up all of Saturday night with a sick or prodigal child.

A friend of mine was rushed to the emergency room with a medical problem. He asked his wife to call the church office and tell them what was happening. Within a few hours word had spread to many in the congregation. But within that same number of hours he was home and well. For weeks afterward everyone asked him how he was doing and seemed to want a full medical report. He found it hard to lead when so many remained focused on a problem he no longer had. He wished he had never told anyone. His stress level was higher from dealing with people's concerns than it was from the medical crisis.

We are complex persons connected to complex social organizations. Our personal lives cannot be independent, and our interdependence compounds the challenges and stresses of leadership.

Stress Management

Stress will never go away. There is no such thing as a stress-free life. Instead of trying to relieve stress, we must learn to manage it in a healthy manner and thus set an example for those we lead. This will increase our own leadership effectiveness. Instead of letting stress take us down, we can use stress to become more effective.

People respond differently to pressures. Some leaders are seemingly unaffected by the daily problems they face. But others have trouble setting boundaries. They allow stress to overshadow the joys of ministry and service.

Stress often builds when we become dependent on the approval of others. We want nothing more than to please people. We long for affirmation, for acceptance. Any criticism feeds our fear and self-doubt.

Overcoming this compulsion involves changing how we think about ourselves. Be ever mindful of God's calling. It is his ministry, and he will provide. Draw strength by focusing on God's will rather than on what people think about you.

It is also important to guard against the common trap of all helping professions: fixing other people's problems in order to find your own identity. Some of us won't delegate responsibilities because we think failure will reflect negatively on us. Other leaders want to do the work themselves in order to get the glory.

Few people will tell a leader to take it easy, so if you find yourself doing more and more to please others, change. Select and train a team of volunteers and staff to accomplish your plans. Affirm these people every chance you get. Enjoy their successes, for they'll do far more than you can possibly do yourself.

The key to a leader's stress management—and it takes this key to open the lock—is to take personal responsibility. Except in rare cases, the leader cannot expect someone else to address, resolve, and manage his or her personal stress. The few exceptions usually involve situations requiring outside intervention— when a family member or employer takes control and forces change through required rest, treatment, job change, divorce, or termination.

I do not mean to imply that leaders are responsible for all of their own stress; they are, however, responsible for the action they take to deal with that stress. The response is the leader's decision—change the circumstance, choose not to be stressed, fight back, resign, use the situation to accomplish positive results. Blaming others may provide temporary relief from stress, but it will come back and cause even greater stress in the future.

Does this mean that leaders can always fix themselves? Or that they should even try? Of course not. The leader may need to hire an assistant, get professional counseling, or quit the leadership position. No one leads in isolation. The very nature of leadership means connection to others. Since others are part of the problem, they should be part of the solution.

One thing we must not lose in stress management is the commitment to personal responsibility. One disabling consequence of leadership stress is the sense of being out of control. When the leader takes responsibility to manage personal stress, there comes a sense of taking control, which may help relieve some of the stress. During a high-stress period in my life, I realized I could not change the behavior of someone whose inappropriate actions were having a serious adverse effect on me. But I knew I had to do something. The "something" wasn't to change the other person but to regularly play racquetball—it was something I could control. Simple? Yes. Silly? Maybe, but it helped!

A group of Christian leaders got together and made a list to "improve health and well-being." Here's what they came up with: (1) Take control of your schedule; (2) Ask for a raise; (3) Invest in friendships; (4) Establish firm boundaries; (5) Get away to pray; (6) Get with your family; (7) Get away for study; (8) Take care of your body; (9) Resolve interpersonal tensions early; (10) Get help when needed.[9] Good suggestions from a group of leaders who were averaging 52.7 working hours every week.

Consider the following practical ways to manage leadership stress:

Take control of your schedule

One young pastor used to say to parishioners who wanted to talk, "Sure, any time, any place." One man answered, "Great. Since I have to be at work around five-thirty tomorrow morning, let's meet for breakfast at four." I was that pastor and I learned a powerful lesson—you don't love people less if you invite them to fit into your schedule rather than trying to fit yourself into theirs.

I also realized that I studied and created well in the morning hours, but after lunch I too often fell asleep at my desk. Afternoon sleepiness was especially likely after very early morning breakfast meetings following very late evening church committee meetings. I was exhausted and less effective because my schedule was helter-skelter. In order to better serve others, better lead the church, and better care for myself, I needed to take control of my schedule.

The first step was to block off morning hours for office work because that's when I did office work the best. The next step was to suggest options when someone asked for an appointment. "Which would work better for you, one-thirty Tuesday afternoon or four o'clock Friday afternoon?" Almost everyone fit into one of the times I suggested. Those who didn't could be scheduled for another time and day. Many were able to take off work or talk on the telephone. Some could come only at night, so I reserved one evening a week for a few appointments. The result? Most of my appointments were scheduled for right after lunch. (I was much more likely to stay awake with someone sitting in front of me talking!)

Taking control of my schedule meant establishing a consistent day off every week. Otherwise, at least one piece of every day would be consumed by someone else's demands. For me the day of choice was Saturday, because that was the day our children had off from school. Besides, most pastors are exhausted (if not depressed) on Mondays, so I decided to be paid for that day!

In a church where there were too many committees and far too many committee meetings, I suggested that all committees meet at seven P.M. on the third Monday of every month. I was available to whichever one wanted or needed me. Committees could connect with other committees. Married couples with spouses serving on different committees could fulfill their committee responsibilities at the same time. It worked well for other church leaders and especially well for me because it reduced my evenings out by 75 percent.

When one couple requested a wedding on May 18, I declined, saying, "That's my wife's birthday. How about a week later?" The bride's father was very unhappy and demanded that his daughter's wedding take place on the date they had chosen. I gave in and performed the ceremony on May 18. Charleen was understanding, but I decided on a new approach for the future. At the end of each year when I purchase a new appointment book, I write down every family birthday, anniversary, holiday, vacation, day off, or other times I want to reserve. When someone asks me for May 18, I open my appointment book and say, "I have a prior commitment on that date. Let's look at some alternatives." Inflexible? No. If there is a good reason to change a day off or otherwise override the system, it can be done. It happens every year when birthdays and anniversaries fall on Sundays. I don't cancel church services; my schedule has to bend.

I'm not suggesting that anyone follow these specific actions; I'm suggesting that we all need to take control of our personal schedules. When the life of a leader is controlled by others, the leader will become ineffective, unrespected, and probably burned out.

Why don't more leaders take control of their schedules? Here are a few of the many reasons: fear of rejection, desire to please, lack of personal discipline, misplaced values, inability to prioritize, unaware that it is okay to schedule oneself.

Take time off

Leaders who work excessive hours and refuse to take time off are not martyrs, they are fools. Even God took a day off.

Employers should know that overwork without rest and renewal will make employees increasingly less effective. Fatigue leads to bad decisions, interpersonal conflicts, resentment, and even death (recent research argues that sleepy drivers are causing more traffic accidents and fatalities than drunk drivers). One physician said,

> I discovered in medical school that the more exhausted I was, the more tests I would order. I was too tired to see precisely what was going on with my patients. I could recognize their symptoms and formulate possible diagnoses, but I couldn't hear precisely how it fit together. So I would order tests to give me what I was missing. But when I was rested—if I had an opportunity to get some sleep, or meditate, or go for a quiet walk—I could rely on intuition and experience to tell me what was needed. If there was any uncertainty, I would order a specific test to confirm my diagnosis. But when I was rested and could listen and be present, I was almost always right.[10]

Wayne Muller argues strongly for the Sabbath principle:

> Because we do not rest, we lose our way. We miss the compass points that show us where to go. We lose the nourishment that gives us succor. We miss the quiet that gives us wisdom. Poisoned by the hypnotic belief that good things come only through tireless effort, we never truly rest. And for want of rest, our lives are in danger.[11]

Among his practical Sabbath suggestions are these: light a candle, practice thanksgiving, bless your children, take a walk, pamper your body (e.g., take a leisurely bath), turn off the telephone (or the computer, the TV, the washer and dryer), seek companionship, surrender a problem.[12]

I guess I'm a little less creative. My list starts with "sleep in." But everyone's list should be personal, whatever will break the routine. For those who do strong physical labor six days a week, the Sabbath ought to be a day of not laboring. For those who are sedentary six days a week, physical activity might be the best way to break the routine. For all of us, the day should include time with God—to catch up on prayer, Bible reading, and meditation.

The Sabbath principle is more important than the actual Sabbath day. It encompasses daily renewal, annual vacations, study days, sabbatical leaves every few years, prayer retreats, and whatever else will provide healing of the soul and body.

One important reason for leaders to take time off and use that time wisely for renewal is to set a good example for others. Leaders are watched in their personal lives as much as they are watched in their public and professional lives. Leaders who do not live out the Sabbath values will infect their followers and organizations with painful and destructive dysfunction.

Decide what is most important

Call them priorities. Call them boundaries. Call them values. Call them strategies. Whatever they are called, blessed is the leader who thinks through them and consciously decides what is most important.

Here is a simple exercise anyone can try. Make a list of all the things you need to do. Ask yourself the question: "If I could only do one item on the list, which would it be?" Go back to the list and mark that item as #1. Go through the same procedure to determine numbers two, three, four, five, and six. Review the list and make sure that if you totally neglected the unnumbered items to complete the top-numbered items, you would be doing the right thing. Agree that it is okay to say no to the less important, if necessary, to accomplish the more important.

Now think through the way you prioritized the list.

- If you had great difficulty deciding, you probably lack boundaries, priorities, and defined values. You may need counsel and accountability to develop these disciplines.

- If you chose your priorities on the basis of pressure from others, you probably let other people define your values on the basis of urgency rather than importance. You may need to evaluate your need to please people.
- If you chose your priorities on the basis of your own deeply held values and the long- and short-range needs of those you lead, you are well positioned to manage stress and to lead effectively.
- If you chose your priorities well but don't live by them, it is time to develop a plan to practice what you believe. In other words, develop new habits and a system of accountability.

Deal with interpersonal conflicts

Every leader faces conflicts. Every leader faces disagreement. Every leader faces criticism. Those who are slow to deal with interpersonal conflicts need to remember this rule of thumb: Talk directly to those involved sooner rather than later. For those who are too quick to confront, the rule of thumb is different: Take time to think through (or write down) what needs to be said to whom; then wait twenty-four to forty-eight hours before talking to those involved.

These simple rules may help:

- *Follow Jesus' guidelines.* "If your brother sins against you, go and show him his fault, just between the two of you. If he listens to you, you have won your brother over. But if he will not listen, take one or two others along, so that 'every matter may be established by the testimony of two or three witnesses.' If he refuses to listen to them, tell it to the church; and if he refuses to listen even to the church, treat him as you would a pagan or a tax collector" (Matthew 18:15–17).

Christian leaders should never be self-appointed, self-righteous judges of others, but they do need to practice and model Jesus' prescription for resolving conflict. One of the reasons there is so little confrontation of sin and resolution of interpersonal conflicts in churches and Christian organizations is because so many leaders fail to follow Jesus' words and do not model healthy conflict resolution.

• *De-escalate.* Ninety-nine percent of problems are like sparks; they will burn out if they are not fanned. The early approach of leaders should be to keep conflicts calm. Once a problem intensifies or spreads to others, it is much more difficult to return to calm, reason, and peace.

• *Use caution when writing.* Whenever you put anything in writing—whether letters, memos, or e-mails—consider the potential consequences before mailing it, faxing it, or clicking the "send" button. If the content is critical or confrontational, hold it for a few days or a week before sending it. Review and revise after a waiting period. Have a trusted and neutral friend read it. Accept his or her advice. Too many epistles are written in the heat of the moment and later regretted. Live with a little more stress today in order to have less stress tomorrow. Never send a letter you are not willing to have copied to others or publicly read. As a leader, your words are fair game for all to see, hear, and judge.

• *Choose your fights wisely.* The manager of a professional boxer turned down an invitation for his man to fight another prizefighter. On paper the deal looked good, but the manager still said no. "My boxer only has so many fights in him, and this shouldn't be one of them," he explained.

Leaders have only so many fights in them. They can't fight every battle. They can't right every wrong. They can't carry every offense. The realities of life and health require that leaders simply "let go" of a lot of situations. Just forgive and forget. Move on.

When a couple decided to leave the church due to a conflict with another couple, I concluded that I would have quit leadership years ago if I ran away because of every criticism, disappointment, and offense.

Some are worth fighting for because they really matter. Most do not. The stress isn't worth it.

• *Don't be afraid to ask for help.* One of the worst mistakes leaders make is thinking they can and should solve problems alone. They have idealized and isolated themselves into believing that they must have all the answers and must solve all the problems—including their own.

There is nothing shameful about asking for help—whether

from a friend, a colleague, or a professional counselor. On the contrary, it is a sign of strength and health to admit weaknesses and an indication of wisdom and courage to get help when needed.

Choose help wisely. Avoid processing problems with all those who surround you. That is a more likely way to compound problems than to solve them. The best person may be a friend or it may be a stranger, but it shouldn't be a crowd. In years of referring people to counselors I have often repeated this simple advice: Develop a short list of possible counselors. Have a brief conversation with your first choice. If you feel comfortable, go deeper. If you conclude this is someone who can't help you, find someone else. Keep doing this until you connect with the right counselor for you. Just remember that the right counselor may have to tell you hard truths, and you shouldn't run or quit because of that discomfort.

• *Maintain margins.* There is white space around the type on this page. It helps you read the words. It leaves space for you to write notes. It looks good and helps you enjoy reading. If the pages were printed edge to edge you would think something was wrong.

We need margins in our lives—extra space, reserves, room for mistakes, order. Dr. Richard Swenson talks about putting margins back into our lives:

> Margin is the space between our load and our limits. It has to do with our reserves. If we're overloaded, we are by definition marginless. Margin goes to nourishing our relationships and recharging our batteries. If we live with no margin for error, when something goes wrong, our lives seem to unravel.
>
> Henri Nouwen said, "Discipline means to prevent everything in your life from being filled up. Discipline means that somewhere you are not occupied, and certainly not preoccupied. In the spiritual life, discipline means to create space (margin) in which something can happen that you had not planned or counted on."[13]

God wants us to be effective Christian leaders who depend

on him and use the resources he gives to manage stress in the context of leadership.

"Now to him who is able to do immeasurably more than all we ask or imagine, according to his power that is at work within us, to him be glory in the church and in Christ Jesus throughout all generations, for ever and ever! Amen" (Ephesians 3:20–21).

Chapter 11

Hope—We Need It to Go On

Story #1

The year I graduated from seminary I became the pastor of a two-hundred-member church in a Colorado community with a population of about twenty thousand. A woman who had visited the church on one or two Sunday mornings called and made an appointment to see me. I was twenty-four years old and inexperienced in ministry. She was at least twenty years older and seemed timid and frightened. With a soft and broken voice she poured out her story of marriage to an abusive husband. I had never heard such tales of cruelty. He completely and ruthlessly controlled her life. She was in frail health, had no money, little church experience, and not much Christian faith.

I listened but didn't know what to say. The sum total of my life experiences, seminary education, and ordination certificate didn't seem to add up to very much. I gave her my best advice but knew it was inadequate even as the words came out of my mouth. Wondering if she might be physically ill, I asked her when she had last been to a doctor. It had been years; her husband refused to give her money for medical care, which he didn't think she needed. In an attempt to do something significant, I took out the phone book and looked up the gynecologists in the community. I made an appointment for her with a physician and asked that the bill be sent to me. I prayed for her and sent her on her way.

Although it was only midafternoon, I left my office, drove the two blocks home, walked into the parsonage and fell on the bed, sobbing uncontrollably.

To this day I'm not sure whether I was crying more for her with her many problems or for myself with my overwhelming sense of inadequacy.

Story #2

Six years later I was the pastor of the same church, but the congregation had tripled in size, had been through four building programs, and was relocated to a twelve-acre campus. Despite the trappings of success, I felt empty. I had already given more than I had within me to give, but the church seemed to have a voracious appetite for more. Then again, maybe they didn't. Maybe it was my imagination. Maybe *I* wanted more and blamed it on them. There were critics, and their criticisms hurt me (though today I can't remember who they were or what they disliked). I knew I could never please them because I was already empty and had nothing more to give.

One Sunday afternoon I sat on the bed in our home and opened the *Denver Post* to read the classified ads. I think I read every ad on every page, hoping to find some job for which I was qualified. My skills and experience matched nothing except entry-level, minimum-wage jobs. My best prospect seemed to be driving an over-the-road truck. I had some experience driving trucks in college, and the pay and benefits might be enough to support my wife and three children.

Story #3

After ten years in Colorado I accepted a call to Wooddale Church in suburban Minneapolis. The church was slightly declining when I arrived, and my coming really helped—the church declined even faster. People were leaving to attend a nearby church that was on a roll. I felt like an outsider trying to get in while others were pushing to get out. Remaining parishioners often reminded me that I didn't measure up to my predecessor.

A man in his twenties came to see me. He hurried through the formalities of an introduction and moved to the purpose of his visit. He handed me pages from Bill Gothard's Institute of Basic Youth Conflicts on "how to accept criticism" and asked me to read them before he began. I took this as a bad omen.

He brought out a spiral-bound notebook with sections of different types of criticisms. He had pages written about my inappropriate leadership. He dealt with my spiritual and pastoral inadequacy. He had a whole section recording my grammatical errors from the pulpit.

When he finished I asked him if he thought my problem was primarily incompetence or ungodliness. After a long pause he said, "Both." I asked him what he thought I needed to do to change. He said that the issues were too big, that I couldn't change that much, and that it would be best for me to leave the church.

For a long time I wondered if he was right.

Needing Hope

After each of these experiences, I needed hope. There is no going on without hope.

If God had not given hope to Adam and Eve, they probably would have quit the human race east of Eden. Elijah was one of the most powerful and effective leaders in history, yet he wanted to die when he became discouraged. Psychiatrist Victor Frankl used his training to determine why some prisoners died or committed suicide at Auschwitz while others persevered and survived. He decided that the determining factor was hope. When hope was gone, people gave up.

In pastoral ministry and church leadership, hope is a major issue. The leader needs hope personally, and the people seek hope from the leader. When hope diminishes, it becomes difficult for a leader to carry on and it is extremely difficult to lead. When people come to weekend worship services at Wooddale Church, I assume they come for hope, not punishment. They have had their share of bad news all week and now they want to hear good news. The gospel of Jesus Christ is the "good news" they need to hear and the message I need to preach. They want to know there is hope. As a teacher and leader, I am to provide healing, encouragement, instruction, and hope so people can carry on. People need to leave recharged for the coming week, not beaten up one more time. Does this mean I cannot speak prophetically? Is it wrong to speak out against sin? Should the teacher not confront? Must the uncomfortable be avoided? The answer is no to every question. However, even prophetic words of confrontation must be tempered with hope. Otherwise we present law without grace, conviction without salvation, and bad news without good news. Like Jesus, Christian leaders must proclaim the message that people "may have life, and have it to the full" (John 10:10). And "Let us hold unswervingly to the hope we profess, for he who promised is faithful" (Hebrews 10:23).

How can Christian leaders keep hope high? What can they do when they lose hope? How can they point others to hope when they can't see it themselves? Where can they find the hope they need in order to pass it along to those who follow? I'm still looking for some of the answers myself. But I've found some principles that have helped me and that may also help you.

Look at the Kingdom, Not Just Your Corner

June 6, 1994, was the fiftieth anniversary of the Allied invasion of Normandy, which began the historic World War II battle to liberate continental Europe from Nazi control. All the major television networks ran special anniversary programs that included interviews with aging veterans.

One of the programs paired two contrasting interviews back-to-back. The first interview was with a marine who landed on Omaha Beach. He recalled horrors that sounded like scenes from Steven Spielberg's Academy Award-winning movie *Saving Private Ryan*. The aging veteran recalled looking around at the bloody casualties and concluding, "We're going to lose!"

The next interview was with a U.S. Army Air Corps reconnaissance pilot who flew over the whole battle area. He viewed the carnage on the beaches and saw the sacrifices on the hills, but he also witnessed the successes of the marines, the penetration by the paratroopers, and the effectiveness of the aerial bombardment. He looked at everything that was happening and concluded, "We're going to win!" Same battle, different perspectives.

Few things destroy hope and distort ministry more quickly than leadership nearsightedness. Always look at the entire kingdom of God, not just one corner of it.

In the heat of a tough leadership battle it is easy to lose hope, become pessimistic, and convince ourselves of defeat. Hope is diminished when we see multiple casualties and repeated loss of territory. But as Christians we must open our eyes to see the view from where Jesus sits. Then we'll conclude, "We're going to win!"

Consider what is happening around the world today:

- In 1900 Korea had no Protestant church and the country was deemed impossible to penetrate with the Christian gospel. Today Korea is 30 percent Christian with over 7,000 churches in Seoul alone.
- More Muslims in Iran have come to Christ since 1980 than in the previous 1,000 years combined. Before Khomeini's revolution in 1979 there were about 2,000 Iranian believers. After years of intense persecution there are more than 15,000.
- Every day in the People's Republic of China 28,000 people become believers. In 1950, when China closed to foreign missionaries, there were one million believers. Conservative estimates now say there are more than 60 million.
- In Africa, 20,000 become believers every day. The continent was 3 percent Christian in 1900 and 40 percent Christian by 1994.
- In Indonesia, the percentage of Christians is so high that the government won't print the statistic; it may be as many as 25 percent of the population. The last official

total of Indonesian Christians, in 1979, indicated that more than two million Muslims had chosen to follow Jesus Christ.

- After seven decades of government oppression in the former Soviet Union, Christians now number approximately 100 million. This is five times more than the membership of the Communist Party at its peak.
- The government of Papua New Guinea has mandated Bible teaching in every school of the country.[1]

Using this list, I added up the number of daily converts to Jesus Christ. It comes to more than 3,000 per hour, 24 hours a day, 365 days a year. Compare this to the miracle on the day of Pentecost when 3,000 people—from many segments of Judaism, including those living among different races, speaking different languages, and coming from a variety of countries and continents—became Christians (Acts 2).

What we consider miraculous when we read the Bible is today an hourly occurrence! The variety is far greater—more languages, more races, from more religions, countries, cultures, and continents. I began to fantasize that one day I would be walking down a street in heaven and a stranger would come up to me and say, "I've heard that you were on earth at the beginning of the twenty-first century when God was doing his greatest thing ever. What was it like? What was your part?"

But that's everywhere else. What about in the United States of America? One of the most widely read, most experienced, and most insightful analysts of the North American church is Lyle Schaller, who writes about what he calls the "signs of hope":

- *The Fourth Great Awakening.* From a broader societal or cultural perspective, the number one sign of hope is what Nobel Prize winner Professor Robert Fogel of the University of Chicago has described as the Fourth Great Awakening. This new religious revival is alive, well, and continuing to spread. It is more visible in the United States than in Canada, more in evangelical Protestant circles than in mainline Protestantism or Roman Catholicism, more in the generations born after 1965 than among those born before World War II, more among

Asian-Americans than among Euro-Americans, more in congregations founded since 1965 than in those organized before 1940, more in pastors born in 1952 and later than among older clergy, and far more in those leaders not in denial than in those in denial.

- *The ministry of the laity.* From this observer's perspective, the most exciting sign of hope can be described in a long sentence. When challenged to be engaged in doing ministry, the laity are responding with enthusiasm and effectiveness if the institutional environment is supportive, if the appropriate training experiences are offered, and if that particular challenge matches the passions, the gifts, and the skills of that particular volunteer. All four of those ingredients (challenge, institutional environment, training, and match) are necessary.

- *The men are returning.* Women have outnumbered men in weekend worship in American churches for at least three hundred years. Since 1944 the explanation has been that women constitute a majority of the adult population, currently by a 53:47 ratio. In the 1960s and 1970s, many congregations reported that women constituted 60 to 80 percent of adult worshipers in a typical weekend. In recent years, however, that ratio is beginning to change. Men are returning! This can be seen most clearly in black churches, in those congregations that project high expectations of people, in evangelical Protestant congregations, in new missions, in congregations composed largely of adults born after 1965, and in those churches that emphasize the relevance of all-male, Bible-study-prayer-mutual-support groups.

- *A new generation of adults.* Perhaps the least widely recognized sign of hope for the future is today's young people in their twenties. Various polls and surveys suggest that for every 100 worshipers in a Protestant church in America on the typical weekend who are in the 70–79 age bracket, there are 160 to 220 worshipers ages 20–29.[2]

Schaller's list of signs of hope also includes new resources available for churches and clergy, the many older congregations deliberately choosing renewal over extinction, a move away from entrenched traditions and toward a new sensitivity to meeting peoples' needs, a growing concern for addressing the social needs of our society, expansion of the number of adults in serious Bible studies, increased roles for women in churches, new inner city churches founded since 1980, and more.[3]

In the United States, approximately 102 million people attend worship services each week. How do you think this number compares to professional sports attendance? Professional baseball, basketball, and football games in the U.S.A. draw 94 million fans per year.[4] That means more people go to church every week than go to professional sports all year. Sports attendance equals about 2 percent of church attendance.

We are in a period of rapid church planting. A prayer movement is sweeping the country. Evangelistic efforts and successes are multiplying. Denominations are being renewed. God is doing something very special in our lifetime.

When I am discouraged and my hope runs thin, I remember that I am part of something much bigger than I am and much more important than the local church of which I am a part. I belong to the church of Jesus Christ, and the gates of Hades will not overcome it (Matthew 16:18). Seeing the worldwide kingdom of God, not just my little corner of it, is enormously encouraging to me. It builds my faith and strengthens my hope.

I believe with all my heart in the advance of God's kingdom and of Christ's church. I am truly excited about what God is doing to build the kingdom of Jesus Christ in our generation. But I'll tell you what sometimes is hardest for me—seeing other pastors and churches succeeding in ways I would like to succeed. It is a matter I continually have to submit to the lordship of Jesus Christ. As a disciple of Christ, I must choose to take delight in every blessing God gives to every pastor, every Christian leader, and every church—whether I am part of it or not. When I do this, I am amazed at the difference it makes in me. The more I delight in the blessings of others, the easier it gets to do so—and the more I do so, the more delight I have whenever and wherever the cause of Jesus Christ prospers.

See Christ, Not Just Circumstances

Hope grows when leaders see Christ and not just the circumstances. Frankly, circumstances have great power over my feelings, and I am ashamed of the control I too often relinquish to certain individuals and situations. One criticism, one setback, one nasty note, one Sunday with poor attendance, or one week's bad offerings can turn me downward and inward.

I have tried to analyze and understand why circumstances so easily destroy hope. It seems to me that dashed hope is mostly a matter of unrealistic expectations. We expect everything to go well. We dream of an ideal church where the best of the Bible's highest exhortations are continually preached and practiced. When we have the slightest setback, we are shattered and disappointed.

The antidote is spiritual. As Christians, our hope is fixed on Jesus Christ, not circumstances. We live by faith, not by sight. We believe that Jesus is Lord of the world and Lord of the church and that the outcome is always subject to his sovereign control. If we don't believe this, we are not truly Christian. But yesterday's faith is not enough to counteract today's circumstances. Faith and commitment must be regularly renewed.

Early in my career I served as a youth pastor in a church I loved. I loved the people. I loved my job. I loved my boss. That's why I was so shocked when after two and a half years the congregation voted me out at a Wednesday night business meeting. I was devastated. It was one of the greatest hurts of my ministry.

The next day the senior pastor was unexpectedly called out of town. On Friday the chairman of the deacons called me and asked if I would preach on Sunday morning because they couldn't find anyone else and they knew I would be free.

I agreed.

Believe me, I thought of many Bible verses to use as texts. I even thought about using the pulpit to get even. Instead I chose to follow old but proven advice: "Teach the Bible and love the people." By God's grace I followed Christ instead of my hurt feelings. That day was a significant spiritual victory for me—a day for Christ over circumstances. It was a day to teach through my actions as well as my words how a Christian can handle disappointment. Never did I dream that two months later the senior pastor would take a new job and the church that voted me out as youth pastor would call me as senior pastor and I would minister there for ten years.

I'm not trying to idealize myself. This is a lesson that I need to learn over and over again. When circumstances are not what I want them to be, I must turn back to Jesus Christ. The church is his church, not my church. These are the people for whom he died on the cross. I serve him first of all and most of all. I am a Christian first and a pastor second. My confidence and hope is rooted in Jesus Christ, not my circumstances. It is when I believe this and live this that I am able to be the kind of leader Christ wants for his church.

Look at Successes, Not Just Problems

Why is it is so easy to focus on problems? After a church service, a hundred people may tell me I preached a wonderful sermon, but if one person says it wasn't very good, I go home remembering the critic and forgetting the praise.

Beware of exaggerating problems and empowering failures. Whenever someone says, "There are lots of other people in the church who feel the same way I do," ask who those people are or assume there aren't any. Be slow to escalate conflict. Most problems need to be de-escalated and handled privately. If you pull the rest of the church into the vortex, you will create an even worse situation. Don't be so consumed with a conflict that you turn it into a church-wide problem.

Throughout Old Testament history the Hebrew people were regularly exhorted to remember successes, not problems. When they won battles, crossed rivers, and experienced miracles, they piled up stones so they wouldn't forget. Whenever they started to grumble and complain, God reminded them of the Exodus and all the other blessings they had received. Every harvest they celebrated the Feast of Booths. Every Passover they rehearsed their miraculous deliverance from slavery in Egypt.

Certainly we cannot gloss over difficulties or leave problems unresolved, but all of our problems should be viewed against the backdrop of God's blessings and our successes.

Wooddale Church has a ministry to other churches called ChurchGrow, which includes three days of mentoring and peer-learning with four to six churches. Each church brings a contingent of lay and staff leaders. We send a consultant in advance to help each church do a self-study. Sometimes we work with churches that have pastors who are discouraged and who confide in me the things that are getting them down. They are very real issues. But then I listen to the laypeople talking about the church and the pastor and I hear wonderful story after wonderful story—reports of changed lives and significant ministry. It's almost as if the pastor is deaf and blind to the good God is doing.

Keep a list of blessings and successes. Thank God for them on a regular basis. Tell and retell these stories in the church. It is a necessary spiritual discipline.

Some leaders keep records. Some make lists. Others save notes of celebration and encouragement to review when they get down. I keep a note in my desk reminding me that Babe Ruth struck out 1,330 times. He set the record for strikeouts. He also set the record for home runs. The reason for both is that he played a lot and regularly swung the bat.

As church leaders, let us admit our strikeouts but also remember and thank God for all the singles and doubles, the few triples, and the occasional home run. Look at the successes, not just the problems.

Look at Reality, Not Just Exceptions

Have you ever analyzed the seemingly perfect models on television commercials? Do you realize that you may be looking at more than one person? The hair belongs to a hair model, the legs belong to a leg model, and the hands belong to a hand model. The voice may be from yet another person. The reason they don't use just one model is because they can't find a single model with perfect face, hair, legs, hands, *and* voice.

Perfection is not reality. Our notions of perfection are generally based on a string of exceptions—the exceptionally good-looking parts of otherwise ordinary people—and the person who looks only at the exceptions and not the reality quickly becomes discouraged. The television viewer may become discouraged because she'll never look like the concocted person in the television ad.

Christian leaders often do the same thing. We long to have

a congregation the size of a megachurch, the good looks of Bill Hybels, the drive of Rick Warren, the preaching ability of Chuck Swindoll, the flamboyance of Robert Schuller, the oratorical skills of Martin Luther King Jr., the creativity of Calvin Miller, and the selflessness of Mother Teresa. No wonder we get discouraged.

What is reality? Reality is imperfection. Most people aren't brilliant. Everyone has weaknesses as well as strengths. Few will ever be famous. But God's grace is for all of us. It is self-destructive and sinful to lose hope by comparing ourselves to impossible standards. Effective leadership is doing what God wants *us* to do with the gifts God has given to *us*. We don't have anyone else's assignment and we don't have anyone else's gifts.

For years I have kept a journal. Occasionally I go back and reread old entries. I once came across a page loaded with grief and pain. The journal entry centered on someone in the church whose initials I had recorded. The situation was too sensitive to risk using actual names. Many years had passed since I wrote that page, but as I read the words the emotions jumped off the page and back into my heart. Strangely, though, I could remember neither the circumstances nor the person, only the pain. The incident that once controlled my life had been replaced by new, more pressing issues. That experience helped me to realize that lost hope is almost always temporary. One of my favorite sayings is "This too shall pass."

Look at Your Call, Not Just Complaints

Although complaining gives temporary relief from the discouragement of frustrations, it eventually becomes a form of self-poisoning. The recently freed people of Israel became chronic complainers during their long and circuitous journey from Egypt to Canaan. Somewhere along the way they forgot that God had called them out of captivity and to the Promised Land. Their complaints drowned out God's call. It was a hope-stealing and fatal mistake.

The call of a Christian is first and foremost to be a follower of Jesus Christ. Any call to leadership or to a specific type or place of ministry is secondary at best. Our call is to be what

Jesus wants us to be and to do what Jesus wants us to do.

Recently I received a questionnaire from the organizers of a conference where I was scheduled to speak. It asked a series of questions, including a few maybe-we-could-use-this-information-to-introduce-him type questions. One of them was this: "If you could be anyone else in the world, who would you like to be?" I thought about it for a while and decided there was no one I would choose to be other than me. Not that I wouldn't choose to be smarter, healthier, more outgoing, more godly, or more articulate. It's just that God loved *me*. God called *me*. There's no one else I could be, so there's no point in wanting to be anyone else.

First Corinthians 12 clearly teaches that we all have different gifts. Just as it is inappropriate for the foot to want to see or the eye to want to talk, it is inappropriate for us to wish we had someone else's spiritual gifts. It is the job of the Holy Spirit to distribute gifts and it is our job to be faithful stewards of the gifts we receive. To know and accept who we are, how we are gifted, and what God has called us to do is truly liberating. Then we can rejoice in God's gifts to others and be content with who we are.

Personally, I was slow to realize God's call. When I was a college student, people told me I wasn't cut out to be a pastor. My seminary professors tried to convince me to become an academic. During a sabbatical a couple of years ago, I worked for a publicly held company in Fort Worth, Texas, and the president took me out for lunch and asked, "Why are you a pastor when you could make a good living in business?" It was an interesting question, because I don't remember any specific call from God to become a pastor. I figured I was called to be a Christian and that call was loud enough. When I first became a pastor my motives were less than noble—I didn't want to go to school anymore, and it seemed like a good idea at the time. But year after year I increasingly realize that being a pastor is what God has wired me to be. Being a pastor is what God wants me to do. Being a pastor is what I am good at. I see myself as a pastor. I really like being a pastor. When other opportunities come along, I don't have much interest in them. They're not for me.

When I get discouraged and my hope dims, I remember the call—that I'm where God wants me to be and that it's the best place there is. When I catch myself complaining—that others are smarter, more articulate, tell better jokes, lead bigger churches—I go back to my confidence in the God who has called me to this place and this task. If I were where those are to whom I am tempted to make comparisons, I truly believe I would be miserable and ineffective. At the same time, I assume that no one is better than I am for the place where God has put me. This gives me hope. I don't have to measure up to someone else's standards. I must be who God wants me to be and do what God wants me to do. And that's a big enough job for me.

This raises a previous and very practical question. What if I'm in an organization that needs something I'm not good at doing? What if the church needs evangelism and that's not my gift? What if the church needs vision and I'm not a visionary?

Leadership is not the charismatic ability of a Pied Piper. Leadership is doing what needs to be done. If the church needs vision and I am not a visionary, I must make it my priority to gain vision. If the church needs teaching and that's not my strength, I have to figure out how to teach. If the organization needs to raise more money and I don't feel comfortable asking for contributions, I need to endure discomfort until I become comfortable asking.

As I mentioned before, early in my pastoral ministry I realized the church needed evangelism. I took comfort in not having the gift of evangelism! Then I came across 2 Timothy 4:5: "But you, keep your head in all situations, endure hardship, do the work of an evangelist, discharge all the duties of your ministry." There is no hint that Timothy had the gift of evangelism, but that's what the Ephesian church needed, so he was told by Paul to do what needed to be done.

My counsel to anyone in leadership is to find out what God wants done in the place where he has put you and then start doing it. If it is leadership, lead, whether you are gifted or not. If it is giving vision, give vision, even if you are not a visionary. If it is evangelism, do the work of an evangelist, even if you don't have the gift of evangelism.

Charles Spurgeon

Charles Spurgeon has been a kind of mentor to me. My parents had many of his books in our home, so I have always known his name and have read many of his biographies and writings. At the turn of the twentieth century he was probably the best-known Christian leader in Great Britain, perhaps in the whole English-speaking world. Yet like other leaders, he struggled with hope.

For a man with so much fame and success, he had his share of problems. Physically, he suffered from obesity, rheumatism, and gout. Relationally, he was often the object of severe public criticism. Emotionally, he repeatedly battled with depression.

How did he find hope when facing these difficulties? How did he keep going? One of his twentieth-century fans says that Spurgeon "viewed his depression as a part of God's plan. His unwavering confidence in divine sovereignty kept him from caving in. He could see that God was using his struggles to keep him humble, to pour out more power through his ministry, and to prepare him for greater usefulness."[5]

The leader doesn't have to be a preacher to face these problems or to choose these solutions. Hope comes from looking at the kingdom, not just your corner; seeing Christ, not just circumstances; looking at successes, not just problems; looking at reality, not just exceptions; and looking at your call, not just complaints.

> Therefore, since we have been justified through faith, we have peace with God through our Lord Jesus Christ, through whom we have gained access by faith into this grace in which we now stand. And we rejoice in the hope of the glory of God.
>
> Not only so, but we also rejoice in our sufferings, because we know that suffering produces perseverance; perseverance, character; and character, hope.
>
> And hope does not disappoint us, because God has poured out his love into our hearts by the Holy Spirit, whom he has given us. (Romans 5:1–5)

When we stop complaining and start focusing on our call, it is amazing what happens. We are set free from having to be like someone else and we are empowered to trust God to do what needs to be done through us, whether we are good at it or not. When we see God bless our efforts, we are lifted to higher faith and greater hope.

Chapter 12

Actions—What the Leader Can Do

AT FORTY-ONE YEARS OF AGE he should have known better, but he recklessly and permanently lost one of the greatest leadership opportunities in human history. His grandfather was the amazing musician-poet King David. His father was the wise and wealthy King Solomon. The armies of Israel were invincible. The architecture of his kingdom was considered one of the wonders of the ancient world. Yet when Rehoboam became king, it took him only three days to make leadership mistakes so horrendous that it cost him most of his kingdom and left a legacy of schism that is still affecting world politics.

The sad story is reported in 1 Kings 12:3–16:

> The whole assembly of Israel went to Rehoboam and said to him: "Your father put a heavy yoke on us, but now lighten the harsh labor and the heavy yoke he put on us, and we will serve you."
>
> Rehoboam answered, "Go away for three days and then come back to me." So the people went away.
>
> Then King Rehoboam consulted the elders who had served his father Solomon during his lifetime. "How would

you advise me to answer these people?" he asked.

They replied, "If today you will be a servant to these people and serve them and give them a favorable answer, they will always be your servants."

But Rehoboam rejected the advice the elders gave him and consulted the young men who had grown up with him and were serving him. He asked them, "What is your advice? How should we answer these people who say to me, 'Lighten the yoke your father put on us'?"

The young men who had grown up with him replied, "Tell these people who have said to you, 'Your father put a heavy yoke on us, but make our yoke lighter'—tell them, 'My little finger is thicker than my father's waist. My father laid on you a heavy yoke; I will make it even heavier. My father scourged you with whips; I will scourge you with scorpions.' "

Three days later Jeroboam and all the people returned to Rehoboam, as the king had said, "Come back to me in three days." The king answered the people harshly. Rejecting the advice given him by the elders, he followed the advice of the young men and said, "My father made your yoke heavy; I will make it even heavier. My father scourged you with whips; I will scourge you with scorpions." So the king did not listen to the people, for this turn of events was from the LORD, to fulfill the word the LORD had spoken to Jeroboam son of Nebat through Ahijah the Shilonite.

When all Israel saw that the king refused to listen to them, they answered the king: "What share do we have in David, what part in Jesse's son? To your tents, O Israel! Look after your own house, O David!" So the Israelites went home.

The outcome is reported in 1 Kings 12:19: "So Israel has been in rebellion against the house of David to this day."

This classic case of bad leadership makes me want to scream, "How stupid!" If Rehoboam had done something different, he might have saved his kingdom.

If he had been fourteen instead of forty-one we might excuse him, but he should have been smarter, wiser, and more discerning. He should have known by then which advisers to trust. The same is true for all leaders. We need to take the kind of actions that enable us to make good and wise decisions. We need to grow and develop into the leaders God calls us to be. Of course, doing this is no small task. But let's begin.

Know Yourself; Be Yourself

My mother signed me up for piano lessons with Mr. Willet when I was five years old. All three of my older brothers had learned to play the piano and the trumpet and now it was my turn. I was excited and motivated. My first lesson went well. I went home and practiced every day. After a few years, Mr. Willet sent a note home with me. It was sealed, so I couldn't peek. The note informed my mother that he was quitting. I was his worst student. A phone call from my mother struck a compromise. Mrs. Willet would become my teacher and take up where her husband left off. She lasted another year before she, too, quit. Unfortunately, my mother was not a quitter. She signed me up with Mrs. Jones, a top-ranked piano teacher aligned somehow with the Royal Academy of Music in London. Mrs. Jones really tried and she really cared, but she quit also. Her surrender came the year I was her only student to fail the Academy tests. After eight consecutive years of weekly piano lessons, I was unable to complete the second-year books and examinations. Everyone seemed to agree that I was not destined for musical greatness and should move on to something else. If only this had been concluded years earlier, a lot of money, time, and embarrassment would have been saved.

It's not that I don't like music. It's not that I didn't want to succeed. It's just not me.

This addresses a critical and controversial element of leadership development. Which comes first, character or conduct, the inside or the outside, who we are or what we do?

A seminary student in Denver told me that he was going to take time off from his education and delay his ministry career to get his life in order. He had decided to "be the right kind of person" before setting out to "do the right kind of thing." I was impressed. I think I even quoted him in a sermon several weeks later. But life and leadership aren't that simple.

There are some things about ourselves that we can change,

and some things that only God can change. But there are other things that neither God nor we are likely to change. Let's face it, God did not wire me to be a pianist. It will never happen and I must accept that. For me to invest time and energy in trying to become a classical musician would be as foolish and futile as trying to make my refrigerator into an oven.

At the same time, it is extremely important that we submit to the transformation of God's Spirit to convict us of sin, cleanse us from sin, and develop us into Christlike persons and leaders in keeping with our one-of-a-kind design.

A key principle is to live out our God-given one-of-a-kind design. How do we do that? Most of all, go with strengths. Millions of would-be leaders spend their lives dealing with their weaknesses and never get around to what they are good at.

One of my favorite questions to ask present and potential leaders is "What are you good at? What do you do best?" Then do it! Don't center your life on what you can't do; center your life on what you can do.

If your weakness is lying or stealing, that certainly needs repentance and reform. But if you are weak at reading and strong at listening, learn by listening. If you are more persuasive in writing than in talking, develop your writing and worry less about talking.

God has created each of us to be ourselves. Discover the way God has designed you and don't try to change that design. Instead, go with the strengths God has given to you instead of focusing so much on your weaknesses that you never fulfill your divine design. Lead from your strengths. Use who you are to do what needs to be done. This is leadership that works.

Be a Lifelong Learner

While listening to public radio in my car, I heard part of a commencement address given to business school graduates of Stanford University. Unfortunately, I didn't catch the speaker or date, but I was captured by the concept. The speaker was asking the question, "How does a business school prepare leaders to run organizations that have not yet been invented?"

How could colleges at the beginning of the century have

trained engineers to design space stations or CEOs to found spin-off computer companies? None of the teachers could have imagined the businesses to come or the leadership skills that would be needed. The same principle applies to theological seminaries. How could mid-century seminaries train leaders for the then unknown phenomenon we know today as mega-churches? The leadership skills required for a scholar are usually different than for a reformer (although Martin Luther seemed to have both).

The answer is really quite simple. Teach students to become lifelong learners.

The alternative, though common, is deadly. Many people learn one way of doing something and then fight as if their lives depended on it to make sure it's always done the same way. History is strewn with businesses, churches, occupations, and technologies, and with people who refused to keep learning and changing.

Consider the changes in education taking place at the turn of the century. Millions of teachers, administrators, and higher education students have learned that the only way to gain quality education is in a classroom with a professor and students. They know this is true because it reflects their own experience. To them, distance education is a cheap and inferior method (perhaps even unworthy of being called education). However, research indicates that there is more student-to-student interaction in a virtual classroom (students on-line with each other from their home computers) than in a physical classroom. Education is about learning, not preserving our favorite methods. Many educators simply refuse to learn a new way. In the past the rate of change was so slow that they could remain in their old ways with relative success until retirement or death. Today they risk consignment to the same storage room with chalkboards, portable typewriters, eight-track tape players, and rotary telephones.

Every now and then you hear the story of someone who suddenly realizes how much the world has changed and decides to learn how to drive a car, use a credit card, send an e-mail, or operate an ATM machine. Most of us are not so courageous or revolutionary. If we don't learn things a millimeter at a time, it is unlikely that we will ever take quantum leaps.

Lifelong learning is more of a mind-set than a regimen. PepsiCo CEO Roger Enrico claims that "a point of view is worth 50 IQ points."[1] Lifelong learning grows out of curiosity, inquiry, hunger for truth, fascination with ideas, interest in people, and personal discipline to choose intellectual exercise over intellectual satisfaction. Such a mind-set is a choice. If you've made that choice, here are a few practical tips to help you pursue it:

Know how you learn

Would you rather read a book, watch a movie, talk to people, listen to others, observe someone do something, or take a formal class? All are valid, but not all are good for you, so choose the one that fits you best. If you are a reader, buy and read books and articles. If you're a listener, buy audiotapes, go to lectures, and encourage people to teach you. If you learn best in a formal classroom setting, sign up for courses every chance you get.

Physical fitness experts advise people to select an exercise they like. For some it is running, for others it is swimming, walking, rowing, or biking. They know that if you don't like it, you won't stick with it. And if you don't stick with it, there is no gain.

Mental fitness is the same. Find the mental exercise you like best and get your mind in shape. Don't limit yourself though. Be willing to test new ways of learning (you might like it). And include enough variety on your learning menu that you choose to learn a little in ways outside of your usual educational diet.

Take responsibility for your own learning

Design your own program. Read your own books. Hold yourself accountable. Go for learning, not a grade. Benefit yourself first of all. Don't depend on your employer or other members of your organization to tell you what you need to know.

• *Ask questions.* Persons in leadership positions too often fall into the trap of always giving the answers whether they know them or not. Using authority to give answers that are ignorant or incorrect is a trip down the road to arrogance. Followers will slowly figure out what is going on, and they will quickly lose trust in your leadership.

In contrast, leaders who request information and seek the expertise of others will be continually taught by others. Others will offer information, tell stories, and explain what you need to know. They will make you succeed.

Ask others what they would like you to learn and know. Ask persons of other races, religions, and backgrounds. Try to get to the place where you can describe their lives and experiences as they would describe them.

• *Listen.*

• *Seek to understand other organizations and systems.* Many times we gain our greatest insights from businesses and organizations that are different from our own. The college president who visits and analyzes other colleges will benefit a great deal. However, there may be equal or greater insight from studying Disney World, major league baseball, or the New York Stock Exchange. When we view information from the perspective of an outsider we often learn more than when we bring our insider's preconceptions to the learning experience.

Each year at Wooddale Church the staff takes an entire workday for an "experience" retreat. Some of the destinations we've been to in recent years are: the county jail (we were searched, photographed, fingerprinted, and taken to a cell); a major teaching hospital (we saw the patient tracking system and watched major surgery); the airport (we toured the control tower, visited the inside of a Boeing 747 undergoing reconstruction, and observed training on the flight simulator); a casino (we observed the patterns and behavior of the gamblers, critiqued the operation of the facility, and ate lunch together); the Temple of Eck, a Mormon chapel, a Jehovah's Witness Kingdom Hall, and the Muslim mosque; a small Christian college and a 2,600-student public high school; the largest Roman Catholic male monastery in the United States; and major local newspapers, including editorial departments and printing facilities.

• *Read.* Read books. Include books outside of your usual interests and specialties. Be sure to read novels as well as nonfiction. Never promise to read a book just because someone recommends it. Ask why, say no, or offer to look at it, but don't promise to read something you don't want to read. Find out about a book before you spend hours reading it. Check out reviews. Learn who the readers are in your organization and ask for their recommendations. By letting them do the screening for you, you can save a lot of time. If you know what a book says, don't make yourself finish it; you're reading to learn, not to complete an assignment.

Read magazines. Choose the few that help you the most. Subscribe to more than you'll ever have time to read and "graze" them whenever you get a chance. At least half a dozen times a year, buy and read a magazine totally outside your usual orbit. Examples (unless one of these falls inside of your orbit) include *Brides, Rolling Stone, Wired, Atlantic Monthly, Ms., George, Fly Fishing, Condé Nast, National Geographic, Southern Living, Chronicle of Higher Education, American Demographics, Motor Trend, Money,* or *Harvard Business Review.* You get the idea. The titles don't matter; just pick something out of the ordinary.

• *Study mistakes.* Periodically make a list of your mistakes and write down a lesson to learn from each one. Then make a list of the criticisms others aim at you and write down (without defensiveness or sarcasm) lessons to learn from each.

• *Pray.* Tell God what you've been learning. Ask God what you need to learn. Ask God to teach you. Keep track of your prayers and God's answers.

• *Add a serious interest.* Gain expertise in something other than your profession (e.g., poetry, gardening, boats, computers, hockey, crocheting, photography, painting, mutual-fund investing, Civil War battlefields, antique cars, early church history, cancer, china dolls, antique books). Become a multi-interest person.

• *Study others in your field.* Watch the old-timers in your field to see how they survived. Observe the pioneers to help you anticipate the future. Learn from the mistakes of others. Learn from the successes of others. Know your colleagues and competition well.

Choose Your Mentors

Mentors are teachers-friends-influencers who shape our lives and leadership more than anyone else. They can make or break us. They show us how to live and lead until we are ready to become mentors to others. According to Larry Bossidy, CEO of AlliedStrategy, "At the end of the day you bet on people, not strategies."[2]

Whenever I think of mentoring, my mind goes back to the classic movie *Camelot,* which is based on the legendary story of King Arthur and his Knights of the Round Table in medieval England. Arthur was a wonderful monarch who loved justice and insisted that might always be used for right. His subjects trusted and loved him. His soldiers adopted his vision and were loyal to him to the death. The table in the assembly hall of Camelot palace was round so that all could sit as equals—not even the king sat in a superior position.

This popular legend has made the name "Camelot" a synonym for the best of everything—the best of people in the best of times in the best of places.

However, like sin in the Garden of Eden, trouble came to Camelot. The two people Arthur loved more than anyone else in the world—his wife Guinevere and his friend Sir Lancelot—had an affair. At first the king ignored the rumors, perhaps hoping they were untrue or would disappear. Instead, they became worse. His dream began to fall apart. Everyone was arguing and fighting, and some were even riding horses into the palace and trampling the once-sacred round table.

Arthur was the king. Arthur needed to lead. But Arthur didn't know what to do. So he turned to his mentor, Merlin the magician. Merlin was already long dead, so Arthur had to go out alone into the forest and carry on an imaginary conversation with his absent friend. In a make-believe dialogue, he asks Merlin what to do and in so doing comes up with the answer.

Although the story is fictitious, the principles contain much truth. A mentor is someone who has taught us so much that we know how he or she would handle a situation even though neither of us has ever actually faced anything like it before. In Arthur's case, he knew Merlin well enough to know the advice he would have given.

Some mentors (teachers) and protégés (students) have a formal relationship. They meet together regularly—once a week or once a month—to study, pray, direct, and reflect. They have lists of topics to discuss, even assignments to be completed. The relationship could last for years or most of a lifetime.

Other mentor relationships are far less formal but equally or more effective. You may choose someone to be your mentor who will never agree to an appointment. You may never personally meet your mentor. The person may have died a thousand years ago. Your mentor may be Saint Augustine, Madame Curie, or Martin Luther King Jr. Whether near or far, dead or alive, get to know this person as well as you can—spend time together, read the person's biographies and writings, observe from a distance, or do whatever you can to "get into that person's skin."

Multiple mentors are a must. Just as it is dangerous to put all your retirement money into a single stock or mutual fund, it is dangerous to allow any human mentor to have too much influence on your life. Pick six or more. Take the best from each. If one falls along the way, you still have the others to lean on. The one who will help you in this year's leadership challenge may not be much help next year, but another mentor's influence will be sufficient.

Good leaders have mentors all of their lives. But the relationships and needs change from year to year. Mentors who shaped my younger years and left an indelible impression have far less influence today. While I hesitate to say that I have outgrown them, I have at least moved past some of them. They served me well for an earlier chapter of life, but not as well for the later ones. Some have disappointed me, thus teaching me what *not* to do as well as what to do. I keep looking for new mentors, especially mentors for the second half of life and leadership. I find myself seeking models who are finishing well, or who have already finished well, because that is something I still need to learn.

Perhaps one of the most important and least understood lessons of mentoring is that the primary responsibility belongs to the protégé. There is significant research on how the very best do what they do. When firefighters make wise life-and-death decisions, when fighter pilots do the right thing, and when leaders make the right choices, they usually can't explain how or why they did what they did. Gary Klein, psychologist and researcher, found that "novice firefighters tended to generate options and make deliberate choices—the classic model of decision-making. But top veterans leaped directly into action. With uncanny reliability, they simply knew the best course to take. When the heat is on, we often just know what to do."[3] But they couldn't explain how they knew. They just knew. Continuing research may help us learn how they knew; how perception, experience, and decision came together in appropriate action.

Mentors may never be able to explain why they are such excellent leaders. They may talk about it, but few have a full understanding or explanation. It becomes the responsibility of the protégé to observe, ask, listen, analyze, and simply get to know the mentor well. You and I may never be able to explain how our mentors did what they did, but we learn enough from them that we know what to do. We know when to pray and when to act. We know when to confront and when to withdraw. We know when to lead and when to follow. We learn it from multiple mentors.

Pile Your Chips

Several years ago I was on a panel discussing leadership, and I used an analogy that caught the attention of Terry Muck, then editor of LEADERSHIP magazine. He asked me to write an article about it, which I did and which he published under the title "How to Win at Parish Poker" (for the record, I did not create the title). The leadership concept is valid even though the analogy seems strange.

Becoming a pastor is like joining a poker game. Although I am neither a gambler nor a poker player, I know that at the beginning of a game each player has a limited number of chips to play with and must use them strategically to win.

Churches generally give new pastors 50 to 100 "chips" to get started. After that, they either gain chips or lose what they have, depending on how well they learn the catalog of rewards and penalties the church runs by (which, of course, no one bothered to tell the new pastor about). For example:

Preach a good sermon	+2 chips
Preach a bad sermon	−8 chips
Visit sick person in the hospital	+7 chips
Sick person dies (was expected to recover)	−10 chips
Sick person recovers (was expected to die)	+40 chips
Bring cookies to monthly board meeting	+½ chip
Lose temper and shout at monthly board meeting	−25 chips

This is just a sampling. The entire catalog is very large.

A friend of mine was called to pastor a conservative midwestern church. He arrived a few weeks early to get settled before his first Sunday. On the Saturday before his first Sunday he gave away the pulpit to another congregation (without asking permission). That cost him 2,000 chips, which meant that if he preached 1,000 consecutive good sermons (which would take roughly twenty years) he would be back to zero. He was done. He didn't have enough chips to survive.

In contrast, another pastor friend of mine forgot a funeral. While the family was waiting for him at the local funeral home, he was eating lunch with another parishioner at a local restaurant. The funeral director called the church office, but the secretary couldn't find him. (He had chosen that day to try a new restaurant.) The funeral director started down the church listing in the yellow pages until he found a willing cleric from some alien denomination who didn't know the deceased and didn't do a very good job. When my friend realized what he had done, he immediately drove to the family home to apologize (by then the deceased had already been buried). The family spokesperson said they would never forgive him. This whole sad story cost him about 30,000 chips. But he had been the pastor of that church for about forty years and had millions of chips in storage.

As you can see, it takes a lot of work to accumulate enough chips to be trusted and followed. Here are some of the rules:

• Credentials (e.g., education, ordination, previous leadership positions, and successes) don't count for much. Chips aren't transferable.

- Chips are easier to win and lose in a crisis.
- Some churches and other organizations are stingy with chips. Some are generous.
- Some previous leaders leave their chips behind for the new leader to use; others come back and steal the new leader's chips.
- Chips must be piled up for significant changes. Never underestimate how many chips it will take and don't squander your chips on issues that don't really matter.
- Learn the chip rewards and penalties by asking, but really learn from trial and error. You may be surprised. Remember the scores.
- Some leaders give you their chips; some take them away when you're not looking.
- Practice Christian stewardship of all chips. They are not to be used for the leader's personal benefit (e.g., prestige, position, salary, office, vacation). Chips are to be reinvested for the cause and glory of Jesus Christ.

It's Not About Miracles

An amazing and wonderful line summarizes the life of John the Baptist: "Though John never performed a miraculous sign, all that John said about this man [Jesus] was true" (John 10:41).

Jesus said, "I tell you the truth: among those born of women there has not risen anyone greater than John the Baptist" (Matthew 11:11). John was a great man and a great leader even though he never performed any miracles.

Modern leaders don't need to be miracle workers. They just need to do what God has called them to do: Tell the truth about Jesus.

Chapter 13

Vision—See the Goal and Show the Way

RUBY BRIDGES LIVED in New Orleans in 1960 when the federal courts ordered the desegregation of public schools. Ruby was six years old when she was assigned to integrate the Frantz Elementary School. The local police refused to protect her, so federal marshals walked her through a mob of protesters every day. They shouted at her. They shook their fists. They threatened to kill her. For one entire school year she was the only child who attended the school. Everyone else stayed away.

In 1960 Dr. Robert Coles, a psychiatrist and Harvard Medical School professor, was studying stress and decided to study Ruby Bridges. He went to New Orleans to interview Ruby, her family, and her teachers. To Dr. Coles' amazement he found no signs of stress. In one interview, Ruby's teacher mentioned that the six-year-old appeared to be talking to mob members each morning when she came to school and each afternoon when she left. Dr. Coles asked Ruby what she was saying. She told him she was praying for them. The psychiatrist found out that Ruby's family prayed together every night for the demonstrators. Ruby's pastor said that when Jesus suffered he prayed, "Father, forgive them for they know not what they do." So Ruby prayed that prayer every day for those who shouted at her.

Dr. Coles could not get this six-year-old out of his mind. Because of the way Ruby touched his life, he began his journey to personal faith in Jesus Christ.

Ruby's story didn't end with the desegregation of southern schools or her influence on a famous child psychiatrist. She had a vision of a very different America and she showed the nation the way to make it happen. On Sunday evening, January 28, 1998, thirty-eight years later, her story was retold to the nation in an ABC television special movie.

Ruby Bridges was a leader, and she demonstrated the excellence in leadership needed for the twenty-first century.

The Vision Thing

Vision is being emphasized and popularized at the turn of the millennium as never before in our lifetime. Even fast-food restaurants have vision statements posted on the walls. The reason seems obvious—during times of change and uncertainty people are concerned about the future and want some assurance about what's ahead. Leaders are called upon not only to predict the future but also to determine the future. The expectation is that leaders will be both prophets and kings. It is a high and unrealistic expectation, but it is the expectation nonetheless, making vision a particularly important leadership function at this time. To admit lack of vision can be tantamount to abdicating leadership.

Vision gives hope. Vision gives the impression that someone is in control. I believe in vision. I think of myself as a person of vision. I talk about vision. I am convinced that vision is a function of leadership. I teach that vision is important to shaping the future of individuals and organizations. Please don't forget these five declarations when reading the next paragraph.

The truth is that we do not know the future. Even the best of futurists merely combine a keen understanding of trends, extrapolate those trends into the future, make some good guesses, and hope they are right. The truth is, we cannot determine the future with our dreams and plans. What we can do is anticipate, forecast, pray, and work toward the future we desire.

Peter Drucker claims that "successful careers are not planned. They develop when people are prepared for opportunities because they know their strengths, their method of work, and their values."[1]

An interesting example comes from the biography of James Dobson, founder of Focus on the Family and radio commentator, whose broadcast is said to reach a billion people. Apparently he claims that he had no vision or plan to get him and his organization to its enormous size and international influence.[2]

Whether talking about Peter Drucker or James Dobson, the message seems to be the same—effectiveness is more a matter of right decisions and hard work than clear vision of the future.

An example of good planning connected to good vision comes from the study of demographic trends and preparing for future impact. For example, at the turn of the millennium the total number of Americans under age eighteen reached 77 million, which is more than at any time in history (including the baby boom of 1946–1964). That means there will be a lot of college students from 2000 to 2018. If they had not been born, no visionary college president could change the demographics. But because they were born and are potential college students, visionary administrators can draft plans to educate and house them. At the same time, the country is moving toward the largest number and largest percentage of senior adults (baby boomers begin turning sixty-six—retirement age—in 2012). It does not take a genius to figure out that we will need more health care, more senior housing, more funeral homes and directors, and more cemetery space. Yet it may take a visionary to make plans that will respond successfully to the millions of new senior adult needs and opportunities.

There Are Only Six Questions

Only six questions have ever been asked in any language, by anyone, anywhere. No one has ever come up with a seventh question! The six questions are "Who?" "What?" "Where?" "Why?" "When?" and "How?" If Aristotle were our teacher he would ask us to identify the most important question of the list.

One of us would quickly answer, " 'What?' is the most important. If you figure out what to do, everything else will fall into
place." Then Aristotle would reply, "Why is 'what?' the most
important question?" Another one of us would raise a hand and
confidently assert, " 'Who?' is the most important question. If
you get the right person to lead the organization and the right
people in the right positions, everything else will succeed. If you
have the wrong people in the wrong places, nothing else matters." Again Aristotle would reply, "Why is 'who?' the most important question?" After multiple tries at other answers we
would all figure out that Aristotle is telling us that "why?" is the
most important question.

To answer the "why?" question, we have to know the reason
why the person or organization exists. Answering why is the
first step in writing a purpose statement. Knowing why is a key
responsibility of effective leadership. An old maxim claims that
"He who knows how will always have a job; he who knows why
will always be his boss." The maxim is an overstatement, but
the concept is important.

Both Jesus and the writers of the New Testament were clear
in answering the "why?" question:

Why did God send his Son?

"God did not send his Son into the world to condemn the
world, but to save the world through him" (John 3:17).

Why did the Son come?

"For the Son of Man came to seek and to save what was lost"
(Luke 19:10).

Why did John choose what he wrote in the fourth Gospel?

"Jesus did many other miraculous signs in the presence of
his disciples, which are not recorded in this book. But these are
written that you may believe that Jesus is the Christ, the Son of
God, and that by believing you may have life in his name" (John
20:30–31).

Vision should begin with an answer to the "why" question.
This is not always easy. Some organizations have no good reason to exist and should be shut down. Other organizations, having lost focus, attempt everything but do nothing well. Honest
answering of the "why" question may lead to revolutionary
change that is more painful than followers will endure and more

challenging than leaders will attempt. However, there can be no
viable vision without a primary purpose.

Purpose statements are a lot of work. Large businesses
spend hundreds of thousands of dollars on external consultants
and internal meetings to craft a good purpose/mission statement. When Wooddale Church developed its current purpose
statement, months of work went into it. We even consulted a
grammarian who helped us distinguish between the implications of using *for* rather than *of*. The result: "The purpose of
Wooddale Church is to honor God by making more disciples
for Jesus Christ." This sixteen-word statement reflects theology
(God-centered), function (make more disciples), and rationale
(*for* Jesus Christ), and it describes our desired outcome (more).

Good purpose statements not only answer the "why" question but state the answer in a meaningful and memorable way.
Here are the tests:

- *Can the statement be memorized in three minutes or less?* If it
  takes longer than three minutes to memorize, it probably
  won't be remembered. If it's not remembered, it probably
  won't make any difference. If it doesn't make any difference,
  it probably doesn't matter.
- *Is there more than one punctuation mark?* Most memorable
  purpose statements have only one punctuation mark: the
  period at the end. The more commas, semicolons, periods,
  and other punctuation marks in the statement the more confusing, contorted, and difficult to understand.
- *Can it be easily explained and understood?* For everyone inside and outside the organization to own and use the purpose statement, those people should be able to quickly and
  simply explain it and understand it.

One of the simplest comparisons is with human organs.
What is the purpose statement for the eye? *To see.* What is the
purpose statement for the ear? *To hear.* What is the purpose
statement for the nose? *To breathe and to smell.* What is the purpose statement for the hand? *To touch, hold, and carry out the
decisions of the mind.*

When it comes to organizations, purpose statements begin
like this:

Christian college: "to educate and to equip Christian students to be lifelong learners and believers."

Relief agency: "to represent the church of Jesus Christ around the world by providing emergency relief and long-term development."

Church: "to please God in this community through Christian love."

These are generic examples. They may be more specific for each organization. And there may be subsequent (and longer) statements that define terms and flesh out the concepts.

All of this is not vision. It is preliminary to vision.

Vision = "What if. . . ?"

Vision answers the "what if?" question. What if Wooddale Church really honored God by making more disciples for Jesus Christ? What would that mean in ten years? What if a college really did "educate and equip Christian students to be lifelong learners and believers"? How would the college function? What courses would students take? Describe their lifestyles for the next twenty-five years. Suppose a relief agency actually represented the church of Jesus Christ around the world by providing emergency relief and long-term development. Would churches have a different role? How would relief and development be connected to the person and cause of Jesus Christ? What is "Christian" about relief and development that distinguishes it from agencies lacking the church and Christian purpose?

Ask the same questions over and over again: *What if the purpose were fulfilled? What if it really worked? What would it look like tomorrow, next year, a decade from now?*

When Bob Buford of Leadership Network reflected on lessons learned from his mentor Peter Drucker, he came up with this list of the top ten:[3]

- The mission comes first. The mission of nonprofits (including churches) is changed lives.
- The function of management is to make the church more church-like, not to make the church more business-like.
- An organization begins to die the day it begins to run for

the benefit of the insiders and not for the benefit of the outsiders.

• Know the value of planned abandonment . . . you must decide what *not* to do.

• liKnow the value of foresight . . . you can't predict the
future, but you can assess the futurity of present events.

• Focus on opportunities, not on problems. Most organizations assign their best resources to their problems, not their opportunities.

• Management is a social function and has mostly to do with people, not techniques and procedures.

• People decisions are the ultimate control mechanism of an organization. That's where people look to find out what values you really hold.

• All work is for a team. No individual has the temperament and the skills to do every job. The purpose of a team is to make strengths productive and weaknesses irrelevant.

• The three most important questions are "What is our business?"; "Who is the customer?"; and "What does the customer consider value?"

Gather these concepts and start developing the vision.

Developing a Vision

What is the usual way to get the vision? Is it for the leader to take a week alone fasting in the desert while God implants it into the leader's head? Does the leader then come in from the desert (or down from the mountain) to announce the vision to the people? Do the people then cheer and unanimously implement the vision? Sometimes it works that way! But not often.

Most visions come from a lengthy process of learning, praying, observing, brainstorming with others, trial and error, rough drafts, trial balloons, false starts, refinement, partial agreement, eventual adoption, and incremental implementation. After the fact, revisionists often try to change the history of the vision. If the vision turns out well, they emphasize the desert and mountaintop pieces of the story. If the vision is a flop, they emphasize the warnings, errors, false starts, and shot-down trial balloons.

Different leaders develop visions in different ways. Some do it alone. Others dream in teams. Many borrow visions from other leaders and places and revise them to fit the local situation. Some envision out of fear and failure while others envision out of creativity and courage. It may not make any difference which process is used as long as the purpose is fulfilled.

What should a leader do? Ask the vision question: *What would the future look like if our purpose really happened?* Start imagining the future. Do it alone. Do it with others. Jot down any proposed idea. List more than you could ever do. Don't worry about words like "impossible" or "contradictory." Address those later. Don't lose sight of your purpose.

The brainstorming stage is easy. Starting the vision isn't hard either. The difficult work is ahead.

Vision is imagining the future you want. Some people want a future exactly like the present. It is a powerful albeit impossible vision to fulfill. Some have a vision of a church just like the church they grew up in thirty years ago. Some have a vision of a megachurch. Some have a vision of a strongly denominational church. Some have visions of rich churches, social-justice churches, integrated churches, cell churches, evangelistic churches, missionary churches, churches with more women in leadership, churches with only men in leadership, liberal, conservative, and just about everything else. Ask any church member what he or she would like the church to look like ten years from now and almost everyone will have a definite answer. There is no shortage of vision.

The challenge of leadership is to gather all the vision from inside and outside the organization, extract the best that matches the purpose, and then craft a vision statement that will unite the people in moving toward the common goal and a more desirable future.

When the vision is refined and explained, the responses will vary:

- Some will not understand. They will need time and teaching and tangible expressions of the vision.
- Some will strongly object. Often they are the people who understand the best and don't like what others foresee.
- Some will quickly agree. They are called "early adopters"

and typically are comprised of 13.5 percent of an organization's constituency.[4]

These principles are universal. They apply to churches, colleges, businesses, Christian organizations, and secular organizations.

As important as vision is, most people don't get it, and vision without implementation is just words.

Showing the Way

Once the leader has the vision, the next step is usually to
give a speech. The leader stands in front of the employees, congregation, or other constituents and describes what tomorrow
will look like if the purpose is fulfilled. The speech must be well
prepared and lavishly illustrated. Even if the leader is not a particularly gifted communicator, the vision speech will be con-
veyed with great passion—because by this time the leader has
dreamed and processed and become personally invested in the
vision. In the best of cases, everyone who hears the speech
agrees with the vision. They may even applaud enthusiastically.
In such cases, the leader feels affirmed, and the vision is off to
a grand start toward reality.

However, that's not always how it happens. Most people
simply won't "get it."

Visions are mostly in the minds of a few leaders. Words in
the air or on paper communicate little more than an introduction to vision because the majority of followers don't compre-
hend it until they begin to see the vision unfold.

Over the years I have been involved in ten church building
programs plus numerous other building projects for mission
and educational organizations. I have sat through countless
hours of building committee meetings; I have reviewed hundreds of schematic drawings and blueprints; and I have walked
across many undeveloped sites. It is exciting to see an idea take
shape at the working end of an architect's pencil. I confess, however, that I have never been able to visualize the proposed structures until the construction has begun. It amazes me that ar-
chitects can "see" what a building will look like before they draw
it. They seem to know how it all fits together and how every-

thing will work. Their drawings are merely a way of communicating what they have already envisioned in their minds. My problem is that I can't get the vision from their drawings—at least not a very good picture of it. Then the ground is staked, the hole is dug, the footings are laid, and the building begins to go up. At last, I "get it." I can see the footprint. I can visualize the building's placement on the site. I can imagine what it will look like when it is finished. The vision in his mind has now formed in mine. Not that everything is finished and final. There will be modifications along the way. But the basic vision is being implemented.

A similar thing happens when leaders have a vision for an organization. In their minds all the pieces fit together. Even matters they have not previously considered become clear when they are asked about them. Everything makes sense. It is almost as if they have traveled forward in time and viewed what tomorrow will be like. The vision is then written into a speech or brochure or letter or book. No matter how well done, very few will see or understand what the leader has seen and understood. The followers will agree because they trust the leader or because a piece of their own vision has been tapped into. But they will never really get it until the vision actually begins to happen. Talk about recruiting students with higher GPA and SAT/ACT scores and most faculties won't grasp the vision until the first brighter students arrive on campus. Talk about making the congregation into a praying church and most members won't understand until they have attended a few prayer meetings and experienced a few divine answers to prayer. Talk about sending retired executives as clandestine missionaries to otherwise closed countries and the idea won't catch on until someone has gone and reported back that it works.

Gary McIntosh offers a short list of what it takes to turn vision into reality:

- What gets pictured gets done.
- What gets modeled gets done.
- What gets praised gets done.
- What gets trained gets done.
- What gets measured gets done.[5]

Leaders themselves must begin to implement the vision. If the leader of an educational institution envisions a multi-cultural faculty and student body, that leader may begin by selling his house and moving to a community or neighborhood reflecting the vision. Or he may switch churches to join a multi-racial congregation. When others from the school are invited to his house or his church, they experience what the leader is talking about, and the vision begins to turn into actual experience for them as well.

Ruby Bridges went to a previously all-white elementary school. She showed people with actions, not words, what it looked like to have an African-American at the Frantz School. Some loved the vision. Some hated the vision. But everyone saw the vision. And it was the beginning of a revolutionary new vision for the entire nation.

This is not to say that the leader alone has to make the vision happen. On the contrary, most visions will never become reality until other leaders and constituents adopt the vision as their own. Institutional culture, values, and action must all change to fulfill the mission. Structural change requires sacrifice. Resources will be allocated differently. Some personnel will leave; new staff will come. All of this takes team commitment and participation.

How Close Will the Outcome Be to the Original Vision?

Do visions come true? Yes. Do they come out exactly the way they were envisioned? No.

Think of a commercial flight on United Airlines scheduled to depart from Chicago's O'Hare airport at 8:30 A.M. and arrive in Los Angeles at 10:42 A.M. The purpose of the flight is to safely transport all passengers from Chicago to Los Angeles. The pilot has a vision that begins at the Chicago gate with passengers boarding. He then envisions the plane door closing, the engines starting, the plane entering the runway, accelerating to air speed, lifting off the ground, rotating, ascending to 37,000 feet, following the flight plan across the nation, lowering altitude when nearing Los Angeles, entering the flight pattern for

LAX, switching to the tower controller for communication, touching down on the runway, braking, taxiing to the gate, shutting down the engines, opening the door, and saying good-bye to passengers as they disembark. It is a vision fully developed in the mind of the pilot before leaving the Chicago gate. It is written on the flight plan and communicated to the passengers over the plane's public address system. But there is a half-hour delay before leaving the gate. A part needs to be replaced. The air is turbulent at 37,000 feet, and the pilot receives permission to fly at 32,000 feet. There is a thunderstorm near Denver, and the Denver Center controller instructs the pilot to deviate 100 miles to the south. Because the aircraft arrives almost an hour late in Los Angeles, the announced arrival gate has been changed from 7 to 23. Did the vision fail? Of course not. Changes are an inevitable part of any vision. Not everything can be anticipated. Leadership requires adaptation and innovation en route. So it is for all leaders in the implementation of all visions.

In the early 1980s Wooddale Church was grappling with issues of purpose, identity, and future. Thousands of leadership hours were devoted to prayer, study, planning, and dreaming. I was the voice for leadership in a Sunday evening gathering to present the vision for the church. I was a little embarrassed by the boldness of what we proposed—new name, new organization, expanded staff, new facilities, and, most of all, a new thrust for evangelistic outreach. I believed in everything I said. I fought to keep my faith up with the vision. Now I have a different type of embarrassment—the vision was so puny in comparison to what has actually happened. When people ask me, "Did you foresee all that this church would become and do?" I have to answer honestly that I did not. I never imagined the thousands of people who now come; I didn't think about starting new churches in cooperation with other denominations; I didn't consider mentoring other churches from around the country on how to fulfill their mandate from God; I never thought of becoming a leading missions church or having extension ministries through a bookstore and radio program. I had no plans to write books. I had never heard of websites. A full-time prayer ministry and prayer pastor were never discussed. Most of the people of vision and implementation were not yet part of the church. The vision became far greater than it started. But if the vision had not begun, the new vision would never have been born. Vision begets vision.

Effective leaders work hard and wisely to implement the vision. Leadership is always work. The good news is that leaders of vision and implementation discover something wonderful along the way. The seemingly impossible happens. The vision grows and takes on a life of its own. Others join the vision, make it their own, and increase it. The idea is soon dwarfed by the reality. What once seemed impossible is history, and a new vision starts to emerge.

The promotional brochure of the Masters Forum at the University of Minnesota is titled "Be the Bee." It is based on the opening page quote: "Aerodynamically the bumblebee should not fly. Not limited by this conventional wisdom, the bumblebee keeps on flying. Be the Bee."[6]

The God who created the aerodynamically challenged bumblebee also made it fly. God is continuing to make the impossible a reality through leaders who have the will to look ahead and the courage to move ahead. If the first bumblebee had listened to the experts, he'd still be on the ground. But God had better plans for him. Good leaders don't settle for what they know they can do; they envision what God can enable them to do. And sometimes it means letting your feet leave the ground.

Chapter 14

The End—Finishing Well

WE ALL KNOW STORIES of leaders who began very well. Their careers soared like rockets on the Fourth of July. People were dazzled with their eloquence and impressed with their accomplishments. But they did not finish well. Many, in fact, ended short of the finish line.

The measure of success is not the start or the middle of the race. It is the end. The way leaders finish the race is usually a result of the way they ran the race. Those who have learned the lessons and followed the principles gain the glorious result of finishing well.

Make Clocks

Built to Last: Successful Habits of Visionary Companies is a study of companies that have outlasted their leaders, raised up new leaders, and prospered for generations. The authors of this bestselling business book, Jim Collins and Jerry Porras, reveal that enduring companies and their leaders are committed to "clock building, not time telling."

They have concentrated . . . on building the company
itself—the mechanisms, the culture, the style, the written
and unwritten rules that make a company go. Focusing on
a product is time telling—a leader may be very good at it,
but once that leader is gone, the company may be left with
no one else who can do it. Creating a company is clock
building—a leader creates a system that can always tell the
time, no matter who's in charge.[1]

In a culture that seeks a quick fix to problems and a fast return on investment, building for the long term is often the road
less taken. However, most contributions that make great differences and outlast the leader take a lifetime to build. Rarely do
churches or other organizations flourish with repeated changes
of leadership. Whenever you study an organization that has had
lasting impact, you will almost always find that it has also had
long-term, stable leadership. One of the reasons is that strength
and endurance are forged in the fire of failure more often than
in the glow of success. Those who flee when problems arise
miss out on the greatest opportunities to lead effectively. I know
a pastor whose strategy was to take a prolonged vacation whenever crises hit his church. To him this was not escapism; it was
a highly effective way of dealing with difficulty. Nearing the end
of his career he advised younger ministers to "get out of town
whenever a problem comes." He spent his career moving back
and forth across the nation, going from one church to another.
Although he was able to help individuals within the communities where he ministered, he left a string of churches with unresolved conflicts and diminished capacity for ministry. He
dealt with everything on the short term rather than the long
term. He knew how to tell time, but he was unable to build a
clock.

Having pastored the same church for most of my adult life,
I am committed to building to last. For me, one of the important
leadership initiatives is the starting of new churches. In 1989
Wooddale Church agreed to start a daughter congregation at
the same time that we were constructing a large and expensive
worship center. Some thought this was folly because "we need
every body and dollar we can have." Instead, the church called
a pastor to start the new work and gave him the freedom to ac-

tively recruit parishioners to leave and begin a new congregation. On the first Sunday, the new church had more than four hundred in attendance. Every two years we repeat this process. One daughter church started with three services and more than eight hundred people.

Seeing the potential to bless others, our next phase of new congregations was to cooperate with other denominations. This may have been the first time in history that a church has voluntarily started new churches for other denominations. Again, the first new church started with significant numbers recruited from Wooddale Church. All of this has been hard work over many years. Preparation for the first interdenominational church took five years.

Thinking about what I will look back on as my greatest delight in public ministry, I doubt it will have anything to do with buildings, sermons, or books. I think it will be new churches. They are like clocks that will keep telling the time long after I am gone.

Remember Tomorrow

A friend of mine explained why older people talk so much about the past when younger people talk so much about the future. He said, "We all talk about what we have the most of."

Certainly it is appropriate to talk about yesterday, but leaders who finish well must remember tomorrow. One of the worst things a leader can do is retire from an organization after the last plan has been completed, the last building constructed, the last mortgage payment made, and the last dream implemented. While this may give the departing leader a feeling of blessed completion, it leaves the organization with a curse.

The leader should always have dreams he cannot complete and visions that will last far beyond his tenure. Then the organization belongs to God, not the leader. Then the mission is more important than the man. Then the people matter even when the next leader takes over. Then there is hope and not just history.

Leaders who finish well are not those who run the last race before the track lights are turned off. Leaders who finish well are those who pass the baton to their successors to run the next leg of the race. Blessed are those who make their successors succeed.

Invest in Others

Hippocrates was the father of medicine and the author of the Hippocratic oath. Until recent years most medical schools required graduates to subscribe to these ancient words. It was a noble tradition of promising to care for the sick without regard to payment and to always heal and never harm. The oath also promises to teach the art and science of medicine to the physician's sons and others to insure that healing will continue long after the doctor is dead. Perhaps that is one of many reasons why so many physicians are the children of doctors.

The old rule of thumb said that a person could have a mentor until age forty and then it was time to become a mentor to others. I think we can have mentors for a lifetime, but the principle of mentoring others is certainly valid.

At the beginning of this book is a list of men who were my mentors. Some have died; some are living. Every day I do what they taught me. Sometimes I wonder if there is anything original about what I say or do; it seems as if everything can be traced back to one mentor or another. The point is that they live and lead through me. Now it is my turn to invest in others what they have invested in me. There are those into whom I have poured my life. They are my friends and protégés. They are the ones through whom I shall continue to live and lead long after formal leadership no longer works for me.

It seems too sad for words to come to the end of leadership and have no successors. It is too happy for words to watch sons and daughters, protégés and protégées continue on.

Trust in Tragedy

Soon after the pastor's diagnosis of terminal cancer, he announced to his congregation on a Sunday morning, "When I came here, I thought it was to teach you how to live; as it turns out, I came here to teach you how to die." He trusted God in the midst of tragedy.

For some, tragedy brings life's greatest leadership opportunities. Leadership seems easy during prosperity and ease. Leaders don't seem all that necessary or important when everything is going well. But when war strikes, when conflict flares, when financial reverses cripple, when morale sinks, when tragedy terrorizes, the leader must trust God and lead well.

Tragedies never come at convenient times because there is no such thing. It may come when the young leader is fired, when the old leader is disheartened, when the middle leader gets sick, or when any leader is on the edge of the long-awaited breakthrough.

My heart was touched by the story of a pastor's family struck by tragedy along Interstate Highway 94 in Wisconsin. Their gas tank was hit by a piece of road debris—a 5 by-18-inch hollow piece of steel bracketing used to hold mud flaps on trucks—weighing 20–35 pounds. The parents were in the front of the minivan. Six of their children were in the back. The vehicle burst into flames, killing five of the children and injuring the sixth. The parents survived. What I remember most was this Christian mother's response when she watched her children die. She said to her husband, "This is what God has been preparing us for all of our lives." That kind of trust doesn't generate at the moment of impact. It had been developing for a very long time. It is the conviction that God can be trusted no matter what happens. It is the kind of trust that enables Christian leaders to finish well.

Jesuit Father Walter Burghardt writes, "Those of you who are ill or crippled can expect to experience, in every fiber of your being, the anguish, the tears, the daily dying, the sense of nothingness that fragile dust can never quite escape. Yet your dust is literally electric with God's own life; your nothingness is filled with God's eternity. Your nothingness has Christ's own shape."[2] This is the profoundly Christian trust that God is the one who leads and succeeds and who does as much through weakness as through strength.

Seventeen-year-old Cassie Bernall became a modern American martyr when she was killed in Colorado's Columbine High School massacre on April 20, 1999. When she declared her belief in God she was shot. Her example has inspired millions to

Christian faithfulness against the worst of circumstances. The night she died her brother Chris found a poem Cassie had written two days earlier:

> Now I have given up on everything else,
> I have found it to be the only way
> To really know Christ and to experience
> The mighty power that brought
> Him back to life again, and to find
> Out what it means to suffer and to
> Die with him. So, whatever it takes
> I will be one who lives in the fresh
> Newness of life of those who are
> Alive from the dead.[3]

Don't Do Anything Stupid

I can't think of a more tactful way to say this: *Don't do anything stupid.* Don't join the very long list of proven and potential leaders who did not finish well because they said or did something stupid and otherwise inconsistent with everything they had always believed and taught.

Adam and Eve led the human race and ate the forbidden fruit. Moses led the people of God and foolishly struck a rock when God had told him only to speak. David led the nation of Israel yet stupidly followed his own lust, committed adultery, ordered murder, and lied about it. They and millions of others have jeopardized or ruined all that God called them to do. They left lasting stains on their leadership parchments. They knew better before they acted. They realized their sin and stupidity after they failed. For one brief moment they succumbed to self-inflicted disaster, which not only damaged them but hurt those who followed them.

The temptation comes in different forms for different leaders, but the top three have always been money, sex, and power. Do whatever you need to do to avoid stupidity in these and other areas of weakness. Form an accountability group. Get counseling. Seek treatment. Whatever. But don't do anything stupid if you want to finish well.

Know When to Quit

Wayne Gretzky's number has been permanently retired from the National Hockey League. No player will ever again wear number 99. It is an interesting tribute to a player described by *Time* magazine as "a most unlikely one." Even in his prime, Gretzky wasn't very fast; his shot was oddly weak, and he was last on the team in strength training. He explained his unlikely success with these words: "Maybe it wasn't talent the Lord gave me. Maybe it was passion."[4] Nicknamed "The Great One," there is widespread opinion in the sports world that he is not only the greatest hockey player ever but that there may never again be anyone else as good. He led the game even though he wasn't as talented as other players on his team. And he led the team to win four Stanley Cups with the Edmonton Oilers and set a long list of other hockey records.

No one asked him to retire; he decided on his own that it was time. "This is not the first time Gretzky has considered retiring; he talked about it in 1991 and 1993. But each time he has proved too talented; even last year, he led the league in assists. But this year [1999] Gretzky has dealt with persistent neck pain from an injury, and though he's the best player on his team, he has seen his skills deteriorate."[5] It was not an easy decision. But Gretzky knew the time had come.

The truth is, there is no formula for knowing when to quit. Most leaders struggle with the decision unless it's made for them by illness, termination, or some other external factor.

Some suggest that leaders should develop at least one other significant interest or skill throughout their career. You may passionately lead an organization but also be good at something else, like running a small business, writing, music, stamp collecting, antique auto appraisals, or spiritual direction. Not only will this help you through the leadership years by giving you the benefits of different perspectives and healthy diversions, it will also give you an alternate identity. One reason some leaders stay too long is that they totally identify themselves with their leadership role. She sees herself as the president of the organization. He cannot distinguish between who he is as a dean and who he is as a person. His preaching and personhood are so enmeshed that it is impossible for him to think of continuing as a person without preaching. When a leader has multiple opportunities for self-definition and fulfillment, there is a greater likelihood of a wise and timely decision to quit.

The external reason is different. It focuses on the organization or ministry and asks, "Am I able to give the best that is now needed?" Gretzky had to admit that he was past his peak. While still good, he was no longer at the top of his game. The team and the sport that he loved deserved better than he could offer. It was time to hang up his skates. Few leaders are able to make this decision without the advice of others. Unfortunately, long-term leaders seldom get very direct advice on this question from people inside the organization. It may take counsel from outsiders or from other leaders who have stepped down to convince a leader that stepping down is the right decision to make.

Christian leaders, most of all, must be careful that they don't stay in leadership so long that they damage their followers and dishonor their Lord.

A Standing Ovation

A young English pianist gave his inaugural concert to a full house in a London hall. His music was brilliant, and when he finished, the crowd gave him a long standing ovation. Young and shy, he retreated backstage. The stage manager urged him to return for a bow and an encore, but the young pianist refused. The manager insisted. "The entire audience is standing and clapping for you," he said, insisting that the pianist return to the stage. "Not everyone is standing," the young musician replied. "There is a gray-haired man in the balcony who remains seated." The manager peeked out. "You're right," he said. "But everyone else is standing. He makes no difference. Don't worry about him. Just go back out there." The young pianist replied, "He is my teacher."

Whether young or old, each of us has people whose praise means more to us than everyone else combined. In our audiences we see some more clearly than others and we always want to know if they approve or disapprove of the leadership we have given.

That's the way it was for another young man whose story is told in the Bible. Stephen was an emerging leader of the new Jerusalem church who took on a very difficult assignment. He set out to present Jesus Christ to a hostile religious crowd. His speech was brilliant, but the crowd turned against him and took up rocks to stone him to death. As the stones hit, "Stephen, full of the Holy Spirit, looked up to heaven and saw the glory of God, and Jesus standing at the right hand of God. 'Look' he said, 'I see heaven open and the Son of Man standing at the right hand of God'" (Acts 7:55–56). Usually the Bible describes Jesus as "sitting at the right hand of the Father," but for Stephen, Jesus stood. Stephen was a leader in tough times—and he finished well.

May you, too, finish well. May you be the kind of leader for whom Jesus stands.

Notes

Chapter 2

1. Comment heard by author at a conference sponsored by Leadership Network in Claremont, California, December 1997.
2. "1998 FACTSHEET: Age and Lifecycle of Existing Twin Cities Churches." Religion Information Resources, John A. Mayer, Director (8851 Goodrich Rd. So. #101, Bloomington, MN 55437; 612–896–0134).
3. Research Services, Presbyterian Church U.S.A., "Presbyterians and New Members: Likes Attract," 1998 survey from website at www.pcusa.org/pcusa/cmd/rs/match.htm.
4. A couple of years later the church needed the equity in the parsonage to build a new building, so the house was sold with little discussion or dissent.
5. For further reading on change and the church see Leith Anderson, *Dying for Change* (Minneapolis: Bethany House Publishers, 1990) and Leith Anderson, *A Church for the 21st Century* (Minneapolis: Bethany House Publishers, 1992).
6. Speech given at "Trendscope '98" conference sponsored by *Current Thoughts and Trends* magazine in Colorado Springs, Colo., March 1998.
7. Jonathan Edwards was an eighteenth-century New En-

gland pastor, missionary, and eventual president of Princeton University, who is considered by many to be the greatest American thinker and philosopher who ever lived.

8. Charles Haddon Spurgeon was a nineteenth-century pastor of London's Metropolitan Tabernacle. His sermons
were published around the world and he was nicknamed
"the Prince of Preachers."

9. Barna Research Group, Ltd., "Survey Provides Profile of
Protestant Pastors," 6 January 1998, from website at
www.barna.org/PressPastors.htm.

Chapter 3

1. Ralph Stogdill, "Personal Factors Associated With Leadership: A Survey of the Literature," *Journal of Psychology*
(1948): 25, 35–71.

2. J. Robert Clinton, "How to Look at Leadership," *Theology
News and Notes* [Pasadena: Fuller Theological Seminary]
(June 1989): XXVI:2, 4.

3. Ibid.

4. E. J. Elliston, "Leadership Development," *Theology News
and Notes* [Pasadena: Fuller Theological Seminary] (June
1989): XXVI:2, 9.

5. Clinton, ibid.

6. Lieutenant Christopher A. Abel, "Answering the Call for
Heroes," *Proceedings* (December 1988): 134. Abel says that
"initially Patton himself was just such a self-made hero. Although the general would eventually be caught up in events
plainly beyond his control, he had determined from the
outset of his army career to be a hero and had worked diligently to accomplish that result."

7. Romans 12:3, "For by the grace given me I say to every
one of you: Do not think of yourself more highly than you
ought, but rather think of yourself with sober judgment, in
accordance with the measure of faith God has given you."

8. The *mission* question is usually answered in the organization's purpose statement. It answers the *why* question:
"Why does this church exist?" It is extremely important for
the leader to clearly know the purpose of the group he or

she leads. If this is not clearly stated or understood, a primary leadership task is to help the organization to define and own the purpose statement.

9. D. James Kennedy, *Evangelism Explosion* (Wheaton, Ill.: Tyndale House Publishers, 1970).

10. This method of evangelism was effective in Colorado at the time. Many people were moving to Colorado from the East Coast and from the West Coast. They were eager to meet people and make friends, so they tended to open their doors to strangers. When this same method was used in Minnesota, it was essentially unsuccessful. Minnesotans seem to have deeper roots and established family and social systems. They are far more reluctant to open their doors to strangers and invite them in to discuss religion or anything else. Situational church leadership in the Twin Cities area meant abandoning this methodology and using completely different approaches to outreach.

Chapter 4

1. Leith Anderson, *Praying to the God You Can Trust* (Minneapolis: Bethany House Publishers, 1998 [formerly titled *When God Says No*, 1996]), 80–81.

2. For a fuller discussion of the theological groupings of denominations see Wade Clark Roof and William McKinney, *American Mainline Religion* (New Brunswick, N.J.: Rutgers, 1987), 78ff.

3. Reginald W. Bibby, *The PCPA Congregational Resource Study*, unpublished (June 1998): 11.

4. Ibid.

5. Ibid., 15.

6. Ibid., 21.

7. Arlin J. Rothauge, *Sizing Up a Congregation for New Member Ministry* (New York: Episcopal Church Center, 1985).

8. Bibby, 11.

Chapter 5

1. "Full time" refers to all employees who work forty or more hours per week.

2. Joe Tevlin, "Report says workers need more family time," *Star Tribune*, Minneapolis, Minn. (April 15, 1998): A1.
3. Based on graphic by Ray Grumney, ibid.
4. Tevlin, A11.
5. Ibid.
6. Ibid.
7. Ibid.
8. Nanci Hellmich, "How much snooze can you afford to lose?" *USA Today* (February 3, 1998): 6D (quoting James Maas, author of *Power Sleep*, Villard Press).
9. Ibid.
10. Ibid.
11. Ibid.
12. Nanci Hellmich (ibid.) writes that "Experts say loss of sleep is cumulative, creating a sleep debt. One hour of sleep loss every night for a week is the equivalent of staying up for an all-nighter" (according to James Maas).
13. "By the seventh day God had finished the work he had been doing; so on the seventh day he rested from all his work. And God blessed the seventh day and made it holy, because on it he rested from all the work of creating that he had done" (Genesis 2:2–3).

Chapter 6

1. John Vaughn, "America's Megachurches" fax newsletter, Church Growth Today—Center for the Study of Growing Churches, P.O. Box 47, Bolivar, MO 65613, phone 417–326–3826 (April 1998).
2. Charles Arn, *How to Start a New Service* (Grand Rapids: Baker Books, 1997), 13.
3. See chapter 8.
4. The criticism of large churches having too many people diminishes with time spent in the large church. Also, those who have grown up in large churches rarely have this criticism and are more likely to feel uncomfortable in smaller churches.
5. One Minnesota pastor regularly told single adults to go to nearby large churches with strong singles ministries, take a

couple of years, find someone to marry, and come back to the smaller church. It actually worked.

6. This may be the most likely day of the year for formerly churched adults to return for a church service. Many churches now have larger attendance on Christmas Eve than on Easter Sunday.

Chapter 7

1. Lyle Schaller, "Twenty-five years later," *The Parish Paper* (September 1996): 7:9, 1.

2. Based on the 1996 statistics of American Church Lists, Inc., P.O. Box 1544, Arlington, TX 76004–1544.

3. Ibid., 2.

4. Ibid.

5. April Witt, "Religion's rebels," *The Miami Herald* (February 18, 1996): A1.

6. Diana L. Eck, "Neighboring Faiths," *Harvard Magazine* (September/October 1996): 38–44.

7. Steve Berg and Sally Agnew, "Spanish speakers are fastest-growing consumer segment," *Star Tribune* (May 5, 1996): A1.

8. Gary L. McIntosh, "FYI: For Your Information," *The McIntosh Church Growth Network* (June 1997): 9:6, 2.

9. Ibid., A8.

10. Leonard L. Sweet, "What in the World Is Going on Here?" *Sweet's SoulCafe*, published by SpiritVenture Ministries, Inc., P.O. Box 3127, Matthew, NC 28106 (March/April 1997): 2:8–9, 7. Sweet's original source is listed as Thomas J. Stanley and William D. Danko, *The Millionaire Next Door: The Surprising Secrets of America's Wealthy* (Atlanta, Ga.: Longstreet Press, 1996).

11. Donald L. Barlett and James B. Steele, "American dream crumbles as jobs head south," *St. Paul Pioneer Press* (September 15, 1996): A14.

12. Barry Dixon, "Rural Route by Barry Dixon," *Atlantic Baptist*, P.O. Box 756, Kentville, NS Canada B4N 3X9 (March 1997), 10–11.

13. In 1999 the exchange rate between the Canadian dollar and

the U.S. dollar was about $.65 making the U.S. dollar equivalent about $30,000 to $32,500.

14. Barry Dixon, ibid.
15. "Tandy Corp. to sell or close all of its Incredible Universe electronic stores," Associated Press article datelined Dallas appearing in the *Star Tribune* (December 31, 1996): D3.
16. Lyle Schaller, "Distribution of Congregations by Reported Average Worship Attendance," unpublished report (September 1996).
17. Hannah Allam, "Battle on the home front: Small store is ready," *Minneapolis Star Tribune* (July 3, 1997): D1.

Chapter 8

1. There are some exceptions to the celibacy requirement. Most notably, married ordained Anglican priests may convert to Catholicism and become married ordained Roman Catholic priests. However, they are not normally assigned to parish responsibilities and are expected to remain single if widowered.
2. Susan Hogan/Albach, "St. Adalbert," *Star Tribune* (July 12, 1997): B8.

Chapter 9

1. Philip Meyer, "Group effort replaces lone reporter of yore," *USA Today* (April 14, 1999): A27.
2. Richard Morin, "We ain't got a barrel of money," *Washington Post Weekly* (December 12, 1994): 12:6, 37.
3. "Blood thicker than . . ." *USA Today* (February 10, 1997): A1 (Source: Brusking/Golding Research survey for Absolut and DIFFA).
4. Charles W. Colson, "Prison Fellowship: A Vision for Virtue," *Jubilee* (January 1995): 3.
5. Peter F. Drucker, *Managing the Nonprofit Organization* (New York: HarperCollins Publishers, 1990), 13.
6. "Teens Outdo Adults in Volunteering," *Star Tribune* (April 24, 1997), E15.
7. Ibid.

Chapter 10

1. Victoria Neufeldt and David Guralnik, eds., *Webster's New World Dictionary of American English* (New York: Prentice Hall, 1991), 1326.
2. Jonathan Kaufman, "For Latter-Day CEO, 'All in a Day's Work' Often Means Just That," *The Wall Street Journal* (May 3, 1999): A1.
3. Ibid.
4. "Personal finances in the parsonage," *Current Thoughts & Trends* (August 1997): 13:8, 14 (article 12293), synopsis of David Goetz, "The truth about debt and salaries," *Leadership* (Spring 1997): 18:2, 85–88.
5. He is also the author of *Margin: Creating the Emotional, Physical, Financial, and Time Reserves You Need* (Colorado Springs: NavPress, 1992).
6. "Margins: Managing Life's Demands" featuring Richard Swenson, M.D., *Pastor's Update Listening Guide* (Pasadena, California: Fuller Theological Seminary, Tape 7014, Vol. 75, 1997), 1.
7. Minnesota Baptist Conference letter to pastors from the MBC Pastors' Council, November 25, 1997, quoting Dr. Archibald Hart in the March/April 1996 *Discipleship Journal*.
8. "Margins: Managing Life's Demands," 1–2.
9. From the Minnesota Baptist Conference Pastors' Council, November 25, 1997. The Council is affiliated with the Minnesota Baptist Conference, 1901 West County Road E–2, St. Paul, MN 55112.
10. Wayne Muller, "Remember the Sabbath?" *USA Weekend* (April 2–4, 1999): 5, adapted from *Sabbath: Remembering the Sacred Rhythm of Rest and Delight* (New York: Random House, Inc., 1999).
11. Ibid., 4.
12. Ibid., 5.
13. "Margins: Managing Life's Demands," 2.

Chapter 11

1. Bill and Amy Stearns, *Catch the Vision 2000*, (Minneapolis: Bethany House Publishers, 1991).

2. Lyle E. Schaller, "Signs of Hope," *The Parish Paper*, 530 N. Brainard Street, Naperville, IL 60563–3199, 1998, 1–2.
3. Ibid.
4. LEADERSHIP, statisical abstract of the United States, cited in *Emerging Trends*, May 1994 (Winter 1996): 79.
5. "Preaching with a broken heart," *Current Thoughts & Trends* (July 1996): 12:7, Item 11268, 16. This is a synopsis of "Charles Spurgeon: preaching through adversity" by John Piper, *Founders Journal* (Winter 1996), Issue 23, 5–21.

Chapter 12

1. Noel M. Tichy, *The Leadership Engine* (Dallas: Pritchett and Associates, 1998), 21.
2. Ibid., unnumbered page.
3. *Star Tribune* (August 24, 1998): D8. Article previously appeared in the *Wall Street Journal*.

Chapter 13

1. Peter F. Drucker, "Managing Oneself," *Harvard Business Review*: (March–April 1999), 79.
2. Wendy Murray Zoba, "Daring to Discipline America," *Christianity Today* (March 1, 1999): 1, 4.
3. "Important Lessons From Peter Drucker," *Net Fax* (July 7, 1997) Number 75 (Tyler, Texas: Leadership Network). Leadership Network's mission is to accelerate the emergence of effective churches. www.leadnet.org.
4. "The Diffusion of Innovation," *ChampionsFAX* (February 23, 1998): 3:4 (Leadership Network, 2501 Cedar Springs LB–5, Suite 200, Dallas, TX 75201). Model developed by Everett Rogers in his book *The Diffusion of Innovation* (The Free Press, 1995) has an idealized distribution of Innovators (2.5%), Early Adopters (13.5%), Early Majority (34%), Late Majority (34%) and Laggards (16%).
5. Gary McIntosh, "Empowering Vision," *Pediatrics Journal*, a journal for the care and nurture of new churches (April/ May 1997): 1.

6. "Be the Bee," promotional booklet for the Masters Forum, sponsored by the Executive Development Center, Curtis L. Carlson School of Management, University of Minnesota, 5620 Smetana Drive, Suite 270, Minnetonka, MN 55343.

Chapter 14

1. Kevin Maney, "Secrets of outliving competitors," *USA Today* (Friday, October 28, 1994): B1-B2.
2. Quoted by Martin Marty in *Context* newsletter (November 15, 1994): 26:20, 4.
3. Charles W. Colson, "Littleton's Martyrs," *Breakpoint Commentary* (April 26, 1999): 3.
4. Joel Stein, "The Great One Skates Away," *Time* (April 26, 1999): 114.
5. Ibid.